"The world's many great challenges are beyond governments to resolve. Innovative thinking and resources will have to come from many places, not least for private sources, including the new philanthropy. Here is your best guide for how to make that possible."

–**Ivo H. Daalder,** President of the Chicago Council on Global Affairs

"*Imagining Philanthropy for Life* thoughtfully reminds us about the transformational power inherent in the act of philanthropy. The authors have also taken us one step deeper into the mechanics of why this is the case and how the impact investment movement is poised to integrate this deeper understanding of philanthropy into a more life-supporting investment model. This level of synthesis is evident across the sustainability sector, and the Philanthropy for Life Initiative gets us even closer to a working model of sustainable investment."

–**Alisa Gravitz,** CEO/President, Green America

"*Imagining Philanthropy for Life* examines with pinpoint accuracy the necessity for aligning our own personal evolutionary process with that of solving the challenges that now threaten our planet and our species. How can we hope to rebalance our use of resources in a "suicide economy" and promote and protect the health of our environment without finding that same balance within ourselves first? Ultimately, those aspirations are indivisible. What this wonderful book makes abundantly clear is that the solution to our larger global issues will most certainly be solved once we embrace change that elevates our perspectives and guides our actions such that we all finally appreciate our place in the web of life as we strive towards that utopian ideal."

–**Bill Sosinsky,** CEO of The Energize Companies

"For anyone who is curious about the value of philanthropy today and for the future, this book is a must-read. It reframes and shapes the way to think about impact in powerful new ways. Integrating heart, talent and focus to create huge strides is inspiring."

–Dr. Donna Hamlin, CEO, Boardwise, Inc.

IMAGINING
PHILANTHROPY FOR LIFE

A Whole-System Strategy to Transform Finance and Grow True Wealth

Dear Marshall & Jane —

May this book serve you in refining your own individual Dharmic Destiny Paths and enhance the satisfaction that comes from the process of giving. All my best,

Stuart

IMAGINING
PHILANTHROPY FOR LIFE

A Whole-System Strategy to Transform Finance and Grow True Wealth

**STEVEN LOVINK &
STUART VALENTINE et al.**

Published by:
Transformation Books
211 Pauline Drive #513
York, PA 17402
www.TransformationBooks.com

ISBN: 978-1-945252-23-5
Library of Congress Control Number: 2017903494

Cover design by: Ranilo Cabo
Layout and typesetting: Ranilo Cabo
Editor: Gwen Hoffnagle
Proofreader: Gwen Hoffnagle
Book Midwife: Carrie Jareed

Printed in the United States of America

In Memoriam

Senator Dr. Offia Nwali

I*magining Philanthropy for Life* is dedicated to Senator Dr. Offia Nwali, who was murdered on May 22nd, 2016, in Ameka, Nigeria, after a life of service to indigenous people in Nigeria and around the world. He was born 74 years ago in the tiny African hamlet of Ameka, when the elders told his parents that he was the reincarnation of the founder of the Ezza people, born to restore all the traditions of the Ezza and other indigenous peoples.

This path took him to a BA at Brown University, a PhD in government and computer analytics from Harvard in 1966, and five years as a global community development expert at the UN. Returning to Nigeria in 1971, he was appointed as Sole Administrator of the East Central State's School Board. There he reorganized the entire school system of the East Central State, which encompassed five smaller states at the time.

He has been credited with setting up the East Central State of Nigeria Data Processing Centre as well as computerizing the Nigeria

Police Force under the Inspector General of Police, Alhaji M. D. Yusufu. With the return to civilian rule in 1979, he was elected Senator and served in the National Assembly until 1983. From then on he worked to persuade successive military governments to create an Ebonyi State that would bring government closer to the Ezza people, succeeding in 1996.

As a member of the National Conference held in 2014, he continued to advocate for a unified Nigeria made stronger through devolution of government responsibilities to the state and local levels. He was given the National Award of Officer of the Order of the Niger by the Federal Government of Nigeria for his services to the country.

For decades Nwali served as the traditional ruler of the indigenous peoples of the Ezza Nation and was at the forefront of the cause of the Igbo Nation. At the time of his death he was the Acting Chairman of the Igbo socio-cultural group known as Ohaneze Caretaker Committee. Throughout his storied career his deep integrity, unparalleled intelligence, and love of humankind attracted a host of followers from Nigeria and around the world.

Our intention is to serve his cause of restoring a global economy of reciprocity inspired by nature and the sacred. *Imagining Philanthropy for Life* is one way we honor him. To support his cause, please contact us at www.philanthropy4life.net.

Table of Contents

Foreword: Hazel Henderson 1

Introduction: Imagining Philanthropy for Life Authors.............5

About the Authors 11

Part I: Imagining Philanthropy for Life NOW **15**

1. The Cosmology of Connection and Transformation 17
   Stuart Valentine

2. Care First – Our Ethical Compass and Light 29
   Louis Bohtlingk

3. Philanthropy for Life – Humanity's True North 41
   Steven Lovink

Part II: Exploring Philanthropy's Past, Present, and Future **57**

4. True Love for Humankind through Time and Space...............59
   Steven Lovink

5. Challenges Facing the Art and Science of Giving...................77
   Steven Lovink

6. Emerging Solutions in Search of True North......................... 107
   Marilyn Levin

Part III: Stories of Transformation of Self and Society **119**

7. A Trojan Horse of Love – KINS Innovation 121
    Susan Davis Moora

8. The Alchemy of Transformational Investing 125
    Stuart Valentine

9. Reciprocity, Respect, Responsibility, and Relationships 133
    Barbara Savage and Jyoti

10. Creating a Care First World 145
    Louis Bohtlingk

11. Spiritual Philanthropy Awakens – Noomap 153
    Andrea Harding and Bret Warshawsky

12. Reimagining Philanthropy as Community,
    Education, and Citizenship 165
    Daniel Blaeuer

13. Reshaping the Field of Philanthropy –
    Flow funding in Action 173
    Marilyn Levin

14. On Philanthropy and Profits4Life 181
    Steven Lovink

Part IV: A Philanthropy4Life Initiative? **193**

15. True North for Humankind Revisited 195
    Imagining Philanthropy for Life Authors

16. Towards a New Era for America and the World 203
    Steven Lovink

17. A New Worldview and Source Code 217
    Louis Bohtlingk, Steven Lovink, Stuart Valentine
18. Ten Ways to Engage with the Philanthropy4Life Initiative 225
    Imagining Philanthropy for Life Authors

Endnotes **229**
Bibliography **239**
Appendix A: The Creation of KINS Innovation Networks 251
    Susan Davis Moora
Appendix B: KINS Innovation Networks – A Primer 259
    Susan Davis Moora

Foreword

Reading this book brought tears of joy to my eyes and warm recollections of my long-time connections with many of its authors.

Frankly, I have had little time for conventional philanthropy as it is usually practiced in the US. I viewed it rather cynically, as a creature of our byzantine tax code, muzzling political expression and dissent. I saw philanthropy as too often in the service of vanity, power, influence, and ego-enhancing "edifice complexes." Mark Dowie's *American Foundations: An Investigative History*, exposed the widespread hypocritical practices and the so-called "Chinese Wall" separating foundations' portfolios from their grant-making programs. This alerted me to all those conflicts of interest. Foundations promoting better healthcare were invested in tobacco and polluting companies. Others were invested in companies making weapons, busting unions, short-changing workers, or outsourcing. Many foundations gave their money exclusively to their donors' alma maters and religious groups. Thus, in all my civic activities and environmental advocacy, I never sought or received any philanthropic grants. At last, in the 1980s, I found pioneer Stephen Viederman, who brought the portfolio of the Jessie Smith Noyes Foundation into full alignment with its social mission.

In the 1980s I focused my activism and books on critiquing corporations and the false values underlying conventional economics, the disastrous financial models of which later caused the 2008 meltdown and tragedies in the real economy of lost jobs, homes, and pensions of millions. My research led to my model of The Love Economy: all the unpaid caring work of raising children, elder care, maintaining homes, and community volunteering proved to comprise over 50 percent of all production, even in developed economies, and often 70 percent in developing countries. The United Nations Human Development Index corroborated this in its 1995 "Human Development Report," estimating unpaid work by women at $11 trillion and by men at $5 trillion, simply missing from the official $24 trillion measurement of global GDP.

How could it be, I marveled, *that all this unpaid production underpinning the officially measured money-transactions in the GDP could be ignored by economists as "uneconomic"?* Crusading to correct GDP has been a lifelong commitment in my writing and activism. This fatal flaw was finally recognized at the European Union's "Beyond GDP" conference I helped organize in 2007 (www.beyond-gdp.eu). The first 2003 International Conference on Implementing Indicators of Sustainability and Quality of Life (ICONS), held in Curitiba, Brazil, was where we invited the Gross National Happiness team from Bhutan for its first public appearance, as I describe in "Statisticians of the World Unite," published by Inter Press Service in 2003.

I kept my faith that both public and private decision-makers would finally adopt all these more accurate, widely available measures of real human well-being. I spent 20 years in the socially responsible investing field, developing similar screens on corporate, social, and economic performance. Finding early collaborators – Ralph Nader, Alice Tepper Marlin, Denis Hayes, Susan Davis Moora – kept up my courage. Pioneers Joan Bavaria, Amy Domini, Robert Zevin, Tim Smith, Geeta Ayer, and Tessa Tennant created new templates.

Today I find accountants are my new allies, co-publishing "Qualitative Growth," which I co-authored with physicist Fritjof Capra, and in 2014 my "Mapping the Global Transition to the Solar Age," with foreword by NASA Chief Scientist Dennis Bushnell, another ally. 2015 saw progress in the UN Sustainable Development Goals (SDGs) and those of the 21st Conference of the Parties (COP21) adopted by 195 member countries. Universal basic incomes I advocated in the 1960s entered public debates along with *The End of Banking*, by Jonathan McMillan; *The Nature of Value*, by Nick Gogerty; and *Financial Management's* 2016 issue on values beyond money.

This book's co-author, Louis Bohtlingk, brought me new hope with his imaginative workshops on Meeting the Mystery of Money. Our collaboration on his *Dare to Care* book was deeply enjoyable and satisfying. My passion in life is connecting highly conscious, planetary-aware global citizens in the many retreats I host at Ethical Markets Library in Florida. What a joy it was to read this groundbreaking book with such brilliant contributions from my deep colleagues Susan Davis Moora, on her KINS Innovation Networks, Louis Bohtlingk's Care First Network, Steven Lovink's deep dive into the history and philosophy – all informing *Imagining Philanthropy for Life* along with Marilyn Levin's deep experience and Stuart Valentine's effort to reform current investment practices toward his holistic vision of the Tree of Wealth. I hope someday to meet the other authors, Barbara Savage and Jyoti on reading their inspiring case studies, Andrea Harding and Bret Warshawsky on their internet innovation Noomap, and Daniel Blaeuer's experience of the KINS network in Florida.

This book is a complete reframing of philanthropy – as it should always have been: love of humanity. This was also the broader vision of Andrew Carnegie, who saw the role of money as community-based and to be returned, adding, "the man who dies rich, dies disgraced."

Hazel Henderson

DSc, FRSA, futurist, and author of many books
founded Ethical Markets Media,Certified B Corporation,
in 2004 created the Green Transition Scoreboard® and the
EthicMark® Awards for Advertising that Uplifts the Human Spirit
and Society (www.EthicMark.org)

Introduction

Imagining Philanthropy for Life Authors

Dear Reader and Fellow Human Being,

Thank you for picking up this book, whether online, at a bookstore, or by way of a colleague, friend, or loved one who passed it on to you. We hope its contents kindle your Promethean fire. May its message flow through that optimism inside you and beyond you to unleash your true love for humankind.

Imagining Philanthropy for Life is a compilation of chapters written by members of KINS for Philanthropists and friends who were invited to do a deep dive into reimagining the world of philanthropy. KINS for Philanthropists is a network in the collection of KINS Innovation Networks (KINS), which teaches a collaborative method for bringing networks of kindred spirits together to address pressing societal challenges through inspired innovative action.

You will learn more about the KINS method throughout this book and in the appendices. As co-authors of *Imagining Philanthropy for Life,* we represent a diverse, multidisciplinary group of experts from the fields of philanthropy, socially responsible investment, venture finance, entrepreneurship, indigenous wisdom, innovation, and more. Each is committed to *transformation of self and society* expressed through our lives' work. You will be introduced to each of us and our stories one by one.

Our book is written for a broad audience of not only practicing philanthropists but also budding philanthropists, those on the fence, and – why not?… every human being.

Today all of us are called on to become philanthropists, as will become clear in the pages that follow. Whether you work at a foundation, nonprofit organization, or government agency; in the corporate world, international development, or banking and finance sector; or are an entrepreneur, this is an invitation to engage your *philanthropic self*. What follows is likely to help connect some very important dots, enabling you to fully align with an exciting emerging future of great potential.

Imagining Philanthropy for Life has been a very rewarding collaborative effort, the main thesis of which is a whole-system strategy to transform finance and grow true wealth. Together we have endeavored to tease out philanthropy's "True North" (its moral and spiritual ideal) as a necessary – if not imperative – set of targets guiding our individual and collective actions on the basis and deep cosmic understanding of truth, trust, and love. True North essentially symbolizes why we human beings are here on Earth and what we have come to experience through everything we do, individually and collectively.

There are three parts to what you will be reading. The "Reader's Compass" below provides an overview of what to expect. You might be quite familiar with many of philanthropy's foundational elements in part II; no worries, you will discover ample food for thought and reflection in the rest of the book, including the proposed pathways presented at the end for mobilizing our philanthropic selves into action.

Reader's Compass

Part I summarizes the outcomes of a dialogue between contributing authors Stuart Valentine, Louis Bohtlingk, and Steven Lovink, who unite their visions for "Philanthropy for Life." They discuss the cosmology of connection, the transformative power of care as our ethical compass and light, and the proposition to embrace the Philanthropy4Life Initiative as humanity's True North. This approach aligns the world of philanthropy with the urgency, need, and opportunity to create an entrepreneurial ecosystem "in service with the whole of life." In other words, an ecosystem operating in harmony with all sentient life.

Philanthropic gifts as private initiatives for public good can and must more adequately provide the impulse within ourselves to rebalance economic, social, natural, cultural, and spiritual sources and "flows" – supplies of money, talent, time, and creativity. Imagining "Philanthropy for Life" by and for all (as in "everybody is a philanthropist" and "we are the ones") indeed needs to become this decade's whole-system strategy to transform finance and grow true wealth.

Part II tells the history of philanthropy, discusses key challenges in the field, and reviews emerging solutions and practices. These topics considered together provide the contextual fabric, facts, and figures for a deep dive into the meaning, purpose, and underlying values of philanthropic activities through time and space. The contours of how philanthropy can be reimagined, reinvented, repurposed, and re-envisioned in the coming decade are explored. This is a timely journey into the soul of philanthropy in response to the urgent call from a deeply interconnected world and universe. Intended to spark transformation at necessary speed and scale, part II affirms the hopeful opening of a window of opportunity to literally love humanity's most pressing challenges into manifested solutions.

Part III presents eight stories about thought leaders putting true love into action on the edges of an entrepreneurial, philanthropic ecosystem poised for conscious transformation and ready to build a prospering, secure, and sustainable world. Each story offers a different but complementary perspective on imagining Philanthropy for Life. They are stories of *transformation of self and society* that are remarkable initiatives for changing our world from within ourselves. Taken together, these stories tease out a bigger story of an emergent "unified field" of being and doing in support of a new wave of reinspired and rekindled philanthropy. Part III foretells a new reality of limitless philanthropic possibilities in which the whole of philanthropy's impact becomes much greater than the sum of its current parts.

Part IV describes why Philanthropy for Life forms the keystone for a new era, restoring America's as well as the world's prosperity, security, and sustainability in the twenty-first century. It concludes with an open invitation to you, the reader, wherever you may be, work, or play, to creatively engage with the organic development, launch, and implementation of a local-to-global Philanthropy4Life Initiative intended to manifest a whole-system strategy to transform finance and grow true wealth. A series of practical steps and options is provided to activate your philanthropic you.

Wishing you life-changing and destiny-changing reading,

Daniel Blaeuer, Louis Bohtlingk, Andrea Harding,
Jyoti, Marilyn Levin, Steven Lovink, Susan Davis Moora,
Barbara Savage, Stuart Valentine, and Bret Warshawsky –
the authors of *Imagining Philanthropy for Life*

About the Authors

Daniel Blaeuer, PhD, is a scholar and researcher in civic-engagement and public-dialogue movements that promote whole-system change. He regularly consults political and civic leaders on strategies for engaging and empowering marginalized groups in the political process. He also consults on how to leverage philanthropic resources within a social and political landscape to create larger strategic goals. (www.Dblaeuer@fiu.edu)

Louis Bohtlingk is Dutch and lives in Scotland with his wife Sandra. He is a trained intuitive and psychic counsellor, certified bookkeeper, and founder of the World Finance Initiative and Care First World. He is author of *Dare to Care* (English) and *Care First* (Dutch). In 2013 Louis started the international, all-generational Care First KINS Innovation Network, bringing individuals and organizations from all sectors of society together in their effort to create a "Care First world." (www.carefirstworldwideweb.com and www.carefirstworld.com)

Jyoti (Jeneane Prevatt, PhD) is an internationally renowned spiritual teacher. She cultivated projects that demonstrate ways of life that honor the Earth and all peoples. As the spiritual director of the Center for Sacred Studies, she co-founded Kayumari with spiritual communities in both America and Europe. Other projects she has helped to convene are the International Council of Thirteen Indigenous Grandmothers and the Unity Concert. She has devoted her life to bringing unity to the planet through alliance-building and collaborative relations. (www.centerforsacredstudies.org)

Marilyn Levin, MSW, is a social entrepreneur focused on catalyzing the global transformation that is under way. She is an award-winning activist, a professional speaker and trainer (www.marilynlevin.com), and the author of *Experiential Activities for a Better World* in English and Spanish. She founded several organizations, including Global Sufficiency Network, GALAXY, and RAY, and served as campaign director for Four Years Go. She currently serves as the managing director of KINS Innovation Networks in collaboration with the Center for Sustainability Solutions. (www.centerforsustainabilitysolutions.org)

Steven Lovink is a visionary, bridge-builder, unifier, philanthropreneur, writer, and outside-the-box change-maker. Committed to building wholes greater than the sums of their parts, he continues his life's journey sensing humanity's emerging future and assembling its building blocks a piece at a time. He is currently working on his forthcoming book, provisionally titled *On Profits4Life – The Alchemy of Money, Love, and Life.* For more information visit www.lovink.life.

Susan Davis Moora, author of *The Trojan Horse of Love*, helped start five socially responsible businesses in media, publishing, and banking. With that grounding in finance, she launched Capital Missions Company in 1990 to evolve the KINS innovation method in the sphere of sustainability. Susan's 40 KINS networks are in social investing, micro-finance, solar, the economic empowerment of women, organics, social venture capital, community-based sustainability, and raising consciousness. For information on KINS and Susan's book, see www. KINSinnovation.org.

Barbara Savage has dedicated her time, energy, expertise, and resources to further the mission of the Tribal Trust Foundation. As an educator, Barbara has shared her experiences with students of all ages, including at the university level. In her capacity as curator for the Santa Barbara Museum of Art Store, she successfully introduced and fostered a market for handmade fair trade products that supports indigenous communities throughout the world. Her company, Showing Up TV, produces documentary films and exhibitions. (www. tribaltrustfoundation.org)

Stuart Valentine, MBA, explores the boundaries of philanthropy and entrepreneurship in his role as director of the Sustainable Living Coalition (SLC), a nonprofit dedicated to Sustainability Education and Enterprise Design. He is also a financial advisor with 16 years in the social-investment, responsible-investment, and impact-investment sectors. The mission of Stuart's Centerpoint Investment Strategies includes "manifesting the experience of true wealth for clients by supporting the integration of their deep life purpose and investment portfolio." (www.centerpointinvesting.com)

Bret Warshawsky and Andrea Harding are a dynamic duo in life and love. Their passions include "integral wealth" and holistic technologies. Their specialty is helping businesses, organizations, and people become more interconnected and integrated, inside and out. They are co-stewards of the Noomap movement/community, a fractal information and communications technology empowering synergistic co-creation and spiritual philanthropy. They work with more than

100 communities globally, engaged in co-developing decentralized, evolutionary technologies and organizations fueled by passion and wholeness. (www.wildwireconsultancy.co.uk and www.youtube.com/watch?v=OWrc214FoAA&feature=youtu.be)

For more information, see also this book's website at www.philanthropy4life.net.

PART I

Imagining Philanthropy
for Life NOW

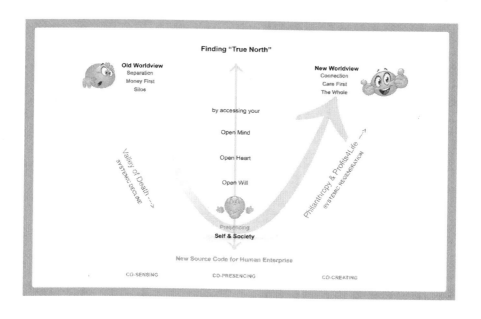

Chapter 1

The Cosmology of Connection and Transformation

Stuart Valentine

Our Cosmic Journey

The act of giving, from a simple smile of encouragement towards another to the laying down of one's life in service of the greater good, is the pinnacle of human expression. We are enlivened and know ourselves more fully through the practice of generosity driven by our experiences of love. The foundations of our cultures and communities are built from the collective process of giving and receiving, motivated by loving relationships. Exceeding even the high status we give to commercial endeavors, philanthropy rightfully maintains the "lighthouse" role in leading human culture towards a vision of a more peaceful union with ourselves, our communities, and the planet.

It has taken billions of years of planetary evolution for the human species to arrive at this moment. And what a moment it is! We are the only species we know of with the intelligence to dominate all other life forms on this planet. While the geological time scale officially has us 11,700 years into the post-ice-age Holocene era, many believe that label is outdated. The human species has so impacted the balance of life on this planet that geologists are proposing that we call attention to our collective impact by naming this age the Anthropocene era: *anthropo* for "man," and *cene* for "new."

Biologists point out that humans have caused an unprecedented wave of mass extinctions of plant and animal species, polluted our oceans and waterways, and altered the delicate balance of atmospheric gases to a degree at which life-threatening climate change is a very real possibility. Indeed our behavior up to now has led us to recognize that to survive as a species we must quickly adapt to cohabitating with the planetary systems that support life. As Carl Sagan reminded us of the consequences of falling out of alignment with deeper evolutionary forces that manage all life on Earth: "Extinction is the rule and survival the exception."

Therefore, to give humanity the best shot at rejoining the web of life we must rekindle the lighthouse of courageous philanthropy with a new cosmology and structure. This challenge requires a top to bottom retuning of humanity's relationship to ourselves, each other, and the planet we depend on for survival. To meet the challenges we face, we must go beyond current market-based solutions and reimagine the practice of philanthropy to better integrate the infinite power and creativity of love.

The journey of reimagining philanthropy must include restoring an understanding of the cosmological principles that govern life. It requires a complete repatterning of behavior here on Earth to achieve a more coherent integration with planetary systems.

This journey starts with stepping back and reminding ourselves that we exist in an infinitely abundant, expanding, living universe. What a privilege to have the conscious awareness to perceive and co-create with this unbounded "field of universal intelligence" we call life! Unfortunately, our collective day-to-day existence has been channeled into a reductionist state of human "doing" that masks the underlying reality of the abundant flow of energy on this planet and our shared unity of spirit. Instead, we are driven by an economic system that promotes a belief in scarcity and conflict. We have forgotten that the universal intelligence of our "being" is continually evolving into a new state of possibility, and that we are, in fact, integral parts of this universal body.

The great awakening represented by the Philanthropy for Life model instills us with the capacity to channel this evolutionary potential into our daily lives. In making these connections within our conscious awareness, we power the collective transformation necessary to realign society with the natural systems that support a flourishing planet.

I Am the Universe

Throughout the cosmos we observe galactic-scale changes continually underway, from black holes vacuuming up matter, energy, and space around them to the birth of stars that give life to new solar systems like our own. From the infinitely small to the cosmically large, all life in this expanding universe teems with vitality and purpose in a constant state of evolutionary "becoming." What we know about this cosmological soup pot of becoming is that there is clearly a body of natural laws that governs the process of evolution equally across all life forms in the universe.

What looks like a seething morass of chaotic phenomena is actually the field of universal intelligence comprised of precise physical laws. As we expand our collective understanding of how these laws govern the universe, we have come to increasingly comprehend that they apply equally to our own internal-change dynamics as they do to cosmological phenomena. The ancient Hermetic principle "as above, so below" embodies the concept that there is a direct correlation between the various phenomena we observe "out there" and our subjective experiences within. Modern science has validated this Hermetic principle via the discovery of the hologram, while mystics and poets have broadcast this principle since the beginning of time. The statement "I am the universe" is literally true.[1]

Establishing this cosmology as the basis of Philanthropy for Life is vital, as doing so expands our *action logic* – the lens through which we make meaning of and interpret events – from a largely egocentric, fragmented process of fixing human problems to one that includes the channeling of universal intelligence into our daily lives. As we grow in our understanding of this "as above, so below" principle, we internalize the reality that the universe is a living system within which we are fully embedded participants. Indeed, it compels the conclusion that life on this planet plays a symbiotic role in the health of the cosmic body.

This vantage point puts us in a co-creative driver's seat with life as we wake up to the fact that the world we perceive "out there" is precisely correlated with our internal beliefs and experiences. The world is as we are, not the other way around. This reframing naturally transforms the "us versus them" experience of separation into the unifying truth that "I am that."

Anytime we feel like victims of events, we now have a framework to use for coming back to the reality that our experiences are of our own creation. This opens the door for a whole new pattern of behavior energized by the recognition that within our conscious awareness is the integral wholeness that we seek "out there." Philanthropy for Life embraces this expanded cosmology as the new source code for sharing a generative, co-creative role with all of life.

The Gift of Life

Given this understanding, one can recognize that we are living in this co-creative dynamic right now, and that our partner, life, is sending distress signals that the partnership is heading towards a cliff! So we are at yet another compelling evolutionary moment in our ongoing relationship with life.

How we respond will determine the future of our species. We thankfully have a globally connected communication system that presents the possibility for a truly global transformation that realigns human affairs into greater harmony with life. To further a transformation of this scope we must create a compelling path that each individual on this planet will be motivated to follow, as we each have something to contribute to the vision of a more nourishing and aligned relationship with Earth. The motivation, of course, is the gift of life we have all received that has embedded within it the design code and the fountain of abundance needed to deliver humanity to this more aligned state.

From the near-infinite number of suns generating an abundant flow of energy throughout the universe, we can be confident that the gift of life is the true central bank of wealth and that there is no shortage of the raw materials of creation. Here on planet Earth, our Sun delivers an overflowing stream of energy sufficient to support all life as we know it. Equally miraculous is the capacity of humans to transmute that energy through our minds and bodies to bring into material reality new structures which reflect that more beautiful world we all know is possible. This capacity drives a never-ending process of creative destruction as we evolve into new ways of being. What was the cutting-edge thinking of yesterday becomes the foundational building block of yet further breakthroughs in design and application. This dynamic is continually powered by the gift of life.

The hero's journey drives a constant creative tension between those who hold on to the old ways of being and those who embrace the evolutionary pull for the new. Philanthropy – the love of humanity powered by the gift of life – is the infinitely renewable battery that maintains this creative tension and inspires human innovation. This is why this cosmological context matters in the reimagining philanthropy process. It helps us reconnect with the understanding that the multiple crises facing the human species are the direct result of a diminished appreciation for the abundance underlying the gift of life and a lack of connection to our cosmological origin. The more we appreciate and nourish the causal field underlying the gift of life, the more we come into alignment with planetary systems that in turn allow the evolutionary engine of new philanthropic innovations to blossom.

But how is it that the human family finds itself in this perceived crisis? We are, after all, of the universe; so how can any human activity be outside the natural order of universal laws? In truth there are no problems, just multiple opportunities to adapt. We are experiencing a state of imbalance because the nourishing power of the gift of life has been short-circuited via our debt-based, profit-seeking, fossil-fuel-driven economic model. The integral wholeness of *Homo sapiens* has, by design, been replaced by the reductionist paradigm of "*Homo economicus*." By evolving from global citizens rooted in the gift of life into mere economic consumer units, we have become the products of an anthropomorphic paradigm that separates us from the fundamental laws of nature that govern sustainable co-existence with each other and the balance of life on the planet.

For example, scientists Joseph Priestly and Antoine Lavoisier discovered the carbon cycle back in the late 1700s. What we understand from this biogeochemical cycle is that life as we know it depends on the recycling of atmospheric carbon back into our oceans and soils. Yet the fossil-fuel-powered economy we have built disrupts this healthy balance, working directly against the carbon cycle by releasing long-stored carbon that the planetary ecosystem is expressly working to sequester. Incentivized by the corporate mandate to "maximize shareholder value," narrowly interpreted as profit, we willingly sabotage this life-supporting carbon cycle in exchange for more cash.

With a global population stampeding towards nine billion, we are collectively waking up to the fact that we must radically realign our world economy with the carbon cycle and with many other biological principles that govern life on this planet, or face extinction. It is a motivating "oh shit" moment if there ever was one!

The path from this scarcity-based, reductionist paradigm that is disconnected from universal principles to one that is grounded in whole-system design is paradoxically not solely an outwardly focused, intellectually driven engineering fix. Rather, the transformation of human behavior must be led by individualized investment in inward attention to cultivate an expanded sensory awareness of, and relationship to, the field of universal intelligence that is the basis of all creation. This field is the source code for realigning humanity with the laws of nature that organize the planetary ecosystem that we depend on for survival.

To transform the limited objective of the profit motive, we must develop an even more compelling pattern of incentives for cultivating behavior informed by the wisdom of life embedded within each of us. It is through transcending and releasing our limiting beliefs that access to this field of universal intelligence can be expanded. The better we are at cultivating and growing this connection, the better chance we have to create the "more beautiful world we know in our hearts is possible," as Charles Eisenstein described it in *Sacred Economics*.

The more our actions are guided by this integrated field of universal intelligence, the more we can give to recharging the battery of philanthropy. Restoring the power of the gift of life in this way drives innovation away from our existing fragmented economic model towards a reward system that integrates our cultural skill of "doing" with the cosmic field of "being." This is the evolutionary leap necessary to get humanity back on the road to healthy co-creation with the universal principles and natural laws governing life on this planet.

Releasing the Old and Allowing the New

Removing barriers to the flow of life that supports creativity in the field of universal intelligence requires intention and courageous commitment to an inward attention. Left to unconscious habit, we fall into fixed patterns of thought. At the core of reimagining philanthropy is the practice of consciously suspending the way we see and judge the world around us to allow for fresh approaches to the art of giving.

By suspending judgment we create opportunities for more penetrating dialogues about the nature of life-enhancing transformation and the flow of love. These "dialogues of one" begin in silence within each of us. Transcending thought and releasing our attention into silence allows our minds to experience the field of conscious awareness that drives the creative unfolding of all life. From this wellspring we bring a greater possibility for connection and wholeness to the philanthropic process.

If our planet and the cosmos teach us anything, it is that everything evolves. As human beings, our highest service to ourselves and universal creation is to embrace this evolutionary process within ourselves. This means making a commitment to continually releasing old beliefs and thoughts and allowing more comprehensive thought forms to take shape. This takes practice and courage. It is not always easy to sit in silence and experience the discomfort of letting go of limiting beliefs. Yet through the dynamic of *releasing into silence* we literally set up the conditions for forging our new beings and, through us, a new culture. Through the practice of releasing into silence arises a corresponding transformation in our beliefs, thought forms, and ways of seeing the world. In this way we progressively generate new, more aligned behavior from the wholeness embedded in our very own conscious awareness.

When we generate a greater experience of transcendent silence within, we naturally enhance our philanthropic impacts by giving from a more unified state of being. After all, if we are truly going to reimagine the practice of philanthropy, we need to harness deeper connections within ourselves that support the releasing of old judgments and habits. This in turn allows for a more life-supporting behavioral pattern and language to emerge.

Committing to True Love

While the field of universal intelligence is ever-present in our awareness, the power of our minds to keep our attention in the domain of *doing* is so formidable that it is easy to go through a lifetime with very little connection to or experience of our own innate states of *being*. The true gift behind this practice is to give ourselves the experience of transcending our minds and opening channels of awareness into the field of universal intelligence. In fact, if we observe our "mother cultures," the matrices of unexamined beliefs that drive much of our behavior, it would be easy to conclude that we are mostly behaving as "human doings." The call to action in this part of our inquiry into reimagining philanthropy is to cultivate a habit of transcending the *doing* and to explore the life-supporting alchemy of *being*. Ultimately we seek a balance between these polarities to drive evolution towards a more whole-system approach to philanthropy, which will be illustrated in the following chapters.

By expanding our awareness into this field, we nourish our whole being, expand our conscious awareness, and grow in our "response-ability" to life in alignment with the laws of nature. An increase in the flow of creativity, hope, and love is the natural result of cultivating our attention in this way, and is the generative inspiration behind the Philanthropy4LifeInitiative described later in this book. The beauty of this approach is that it empowers us with the courage to take meaningful responsibility for the transformation we seek "out there" by more comprehensively informing our external actions through a deepening connection to universal intelligence at the base of our being.

This generative polarity wakes up the recognition that we are all intimately capable of transforming our individual AND collective condition into one that harmonizes with planetary ecosystems and universal intelligence. Our Philanthropy for Life call to action is clear: to release ourselves into the gift of life and co-create the new. We have the cosmological road map and the universal principle of "as above, so below" to guide us. Let's give it our best!

Chapter 2

Care First –
Our Ethical Compass and Light

Louis Bohtlingk

"Care First" is a concept introduced in my book *Dare to Care: A Love-Based Foundation for Money and Finance.* In a "Care First world," money serves the well-being of people and the Earth, and is not used at their expense, which I define as "Money First."

Hazel Henderson – author, independent futurist, and worldwide syndicated columnist – assisted me with the writing of *Dare to Care.* She coined the phrase "The Love Economy" in the 1960s, describing an economy of the heart. Let's add "the love-based economy" and "the love-based use of money" to this, in which love guides every aspect of commerce and creates a new foundation for finance and economics for generations to come.

In her article "The Economy of Care," the Dutch economist Thera van Osch described this theory as the movement from "*Homo economicus*" to "the caring human being." She discusses the "Ethics of Care," which stem from the feminist movement and are recognized in economics research.[1] Building on these Ethics of Care, van Osch created a picture of what an "Economy of Care" looks like: care as the underpinning of all financial, economic, social, and cultural actions – of all aspects of our lives.

Bridging Above and Below with Care First

The application of Care First can be seen as a bridge integrating the principle "as above, so below" into our hearts, minds, and spirits. Our innate capacity to care grows out of cultivating the connection between heart, mind, and spirit, and is the power within our core selves and higher beings. Exercising this level of caring in our daily lives deeply influences both our emotional and intellectual relationships with money. Imagine the collective outcome in our economies and cultures if we each committed to a Care First ethic informed by the intelligence of nature.

To listen to that inner voice of caring takes the discipline of stillness and the feeling sense of the heart, where we experience the care for ourselves, for each other, and for our beautiful planet Earth.

This quality of caring naturally bridges the causal field of our internal beliefs and emotions to the outer effects we experience in daily life. It manifests our highest aspirations into our daily lives. Many great achievements in service of the well-being of people and the planet were the result of the application of caring powered by universal love. What will matter to us on our deathbeds as the most significant moments in our lives? Will they be the courageous actions we took expressing our deepest love for ourselves and others?

When money and finance serve the care of ourselves, each other, and our planet, we return home to the world of our true nature and deepest dreams. From that foundation we create what we long for: a love-based economy that generates a Care First society. A society that reflects our highest vision of heaven on Earth is like a healthy garden in which each individual is fully expressed within themselves and engaged in vital community relationships. So what does this garden look and feel like?

What Is the Garden?

In the Garden we stand together
with the presence of love in our hearts.
We are in community and co-create our dreams.
We hold each other, ourselves and all life on this planet
in love's embrace.
We are present with that love and live that love.
We connect heaven and earth,
work with spirit and matter in their perfect marriage.
We are happy and fulfill our soul's calling.
We serve the greater good,
the evolution of ourselves, each other and our planet.
In the Garden we are at peace.

We experience the Mystery, we are ourselves, and have each other.
In the Garden our souls can rest
in a world of love, where justice prevails.
It is the manifestation of our deepest dream.
In the Garden we live that dream.
We do not wait for it to happen.
We put love in action.
We apply Care First.
We create a beautiful world.

(from *Dare to Care* by Louis Bohtlingk)

The Choice between Money First and Care First

When we take hold of a dollar and visualize it doing what care and love would do, we see beautiful things happen. This is the world of Care First. Money First and Care First are two aspects of testing our commitment to building a Care First world. Let's look more closely at the theories of Care First and Money First to see how we can clarify our concepts and decisions regarding money.

- In a Care First economy, we use money in service of our caring, our values, and our passions. We use money in service of the well-being of people and the Earth. We create a flow of finance that heals all it touches, unites us, and creates a world of love. Care First creates truth and a love-based economy.

- In a Money First economy, we use money at the *expense* of our caring, our values, and our passions. We use money at the expense of the well-being of people and the Earth. We create a flow of finance that destroys all it touches, separates us, and creates a world of fear. Money First creates illusion and a fear-based economy.

- As we enter the Money First aspect of our lives and cultures, we move into illusion. We strive for money while sacrificing empathy, life, and spirit, hoping to find fulfillment but instead being left with feelings of emptiness. This can lead to anger and frustration and can open the apathetic and destructive sides of our natures.

- As we enter the Care First aspect of our lives and cultures, we experience the deep truths of ourselves and nature. When Care First is our goal and money is used to serve that aim, we create fullness. This leads to satisfaction and happiness and opens the caring and constructive sides of our natures.

Can you see what will happen when we help each other move from Money First to Care First?

Envisioning a Care First World

When every economic entity serves the well-being of people and the Earth on all levels (material, emotional, mental, and spiritual), we are healing ourselves and all living things on our planet. This is the path of Care First. In this sense our world economy consists of two parts: a Money First economy and a Care First economy; or as author and activist David Korten puts it: a "suicide economy" and a "living economy."[2] In our own personal psyches and as a culture we constantly move in and out of both. We constantly choose between these modes of operating, whether we are conscious of it or not.

When we live with the intention of Care First, we address the issues in our lives, communities, and world without fear of scarcity. The Care First mentality manifests the flow of finance, resources, and events for balanced sustainability. Becoming clear about the illusions of Money First and the power of the Care First approach – the process of money serving universal love – allows for a real breakthrough of caring in the world.

Money itself doesn't make us happy. It is only a tool we use to achieve joy. It is a movement or flow of energy that can bless the world. But we do not need to be attached to it. We can be inwardly free with it, and we can serve with money. We can connect to each other through money instead of allowing it to create separation. We can create peace instead of war with it, and harmony instead of conflict. Money can be a powerful tool for creating a caring world.

When we live in the mode of Money First, we are tense, alone, separated, fearful, and depressed. When we live in the mode of Care First, we are strong, vibrant, happy, and, most important, in harmony with ourselves.

Let's consider a Care First world vision. Can you see what happens when our conflicts regarding money resolve? People lose their defensiveness and fear about money and work together to support one another with it. Can you see the effusion of money imbued by love and care beginning to flow everywhere? Can you see this new dance, this new release, this new horizon? And isn't it natural and inevitable for us all to go there? The human soul cannot bear being contracted around money, work, and survival, nor can it live with a sense of separation for very long. We seek love and unity. So how can this be applied?

I suggest we ask ourselves:

- Do we put money before caring or caring before money in our financial decision-making?

- Do we create systems and mechanisms that prevent us from applying the Care First experience, and if so can we change and improve the system to facilitate the conscious practice of Care First and serve humankind and the Earth in a better way?

- How does the Care First concept apply to money in our personal lives? Where are we on the Care First – Money First continuum, and what steps can we take towards Care First, if that is what we aspire to?

- These questions can be asked by anyone in this world in any situation and in any service or position. Each one of us can think and live in a state of Care First consciousness every day, if we choose to.

Daring to Care

The current paradigm is all about finance and competition. When you compete successfully, you are a big shot. To redefine the idea of courage as caring, "dare to care" deeply speaks to me. It is the truth. It is more courageous to care than not to care, which in itself is pretty easy.
–Hazel Henderson,
from an interview with me about *Dare to Care*

The Care First paradigm always calls up the highest morality and the greatest care for people. It is so important that we learn to listen to the language of our hearts and understand their power and intelligence – to listen to the cores of our beings (our hearts of hearts). It takes courage to go there – to overcome our fears and conditioning and break through social pressures in relation to how we live with money.

We live in a world in which it is not easy to live in a Care First manner, and Money First governs many things. We can make breakthroughs in ourselves and as a culture so that care truly leads the way in all things. This is what my book *Dare to Care* is about.

The change begins with us – with our attitudes, responsibility, and consciousness. Money First and Care First are attitudes that influence our decisions as individuals at every level of decision-making in our culture. We can all support each through daring to care.

Supporting Each Other with Love and Compassion

The choices we make about money can be embraced by love and compassion for ourselves and each other. We can perceive the consequences of our behavior with money and determine whether we build or destroy our lives and cultures, heal or hurt others, and take energy from or give it to our communities. We can support each other in approaching life from the Care First perspective, if we wish. We can ask ourselves individually and as communities to live consciously and responsibly together. Let us also do this without negative judgment towards ourselves and others, and behave with love and compassion, knowing that we rise and fall together and that none of us is better than the other. We are equal in a universe propelled by love.

We are collectively moving through the spectrum of human experience from fear, greed, possessiveness, selfishness, and desire for power to caring, sharing, loving, giving, and receiving; from a Money First consciousness to a Care First consciousness. We are all in it together and can support each other in whatever transitions we wish to make.

On Care, Philanthropy, and Life

When philanthropy embraces life, it expands the horizon. I see philanthropy celebrating life as the full expression of love-based intelligence in action. In the creation, allocation, and use of money, it is in the application of Care First rather than Money First that we move from using money at the expense of the well-being of people and planet towards using it in service of that well-being.

What van Osch's vision of an Economy of Care and my vision of a Care First world have in common is the understanding that all problems are caused by a lack of caring and resolve themselves through conscious caring. This is what we are building into the foundations of our clarion call to embrace Philanthropy for Life.

How can the concept of caring best be applied to both philanthropy and life? The highest level of philanthropy naturally empowers people to be comfortable with their true selves, give their best, and become self-sufficient. It supports the creation of a prospering world in which both people and nature flourish. I see this empowerment happening to both the giver and the recipient. They can become unified in the process of serving the cause together.

We are defining Philanthropy for Life as being in service with all life, all stakeholders, and the well-being of all people and the planet. We can ensure that money, throughout the processes of gifting, investing, running a business, making profits, and allocating those profits, serves the well-being of all stakeholders. This applies to every kind of exchange, be it monetary, complementary, or with no currency changing hands.

Frits Goldschmeding, founder of the worldwide employment agency Randstad, stated that since the agency was founded in 1960 it had been their policy to consider all stakeholders in the decisions they made. He knows that it is not the easiest thing to do, but believes in it for the benefit of and service to all parties. He is the richest man in the Netherlands, but lives a humble and simple life. He created the Goldschmeding Foundation in 2016 to use his wealth to bring love and humaneness into the economy. The foundation's leading principle is love – *agape* – which is described as "asking ourselves how to act in the best interest of our fellow human beings for the promotion of a more humane society." For more information about The Goldschmeding Foundation and its fascinating work, visit their website: https://goldschmedingfoundation.org.

It is such a step forward in our evolution that someone like Frits Goldschmeding, after 50 years of leading a very successful business life, puts all his energy into bringing love to the foundations of our economies. He is a professor at the Centre for Entrepreneurship at Nyenrode Business University, and hopes to fund the development of holistic education in economic matters.

The Significance of Love

A love-based economy and a love-based use of money can open up a whole new path for humanity in harmony with the whole of life. We struggle with love. We instinctively think of emotional love, which isn't necessarily real love. Love, which can be the foundation for finance and for our economies, is a core experience of the self. Love can be seen as the substance of our universe – the all-pervasive field of energy that guides all we do and all we are. When we feel fear, or the constriction that comes from fear, we are not "breathing into" love.

In a fear-based economy and with a fear-based relationship to money, many of us experience this constriction and a subsequent lack of fulfillment. From fear it is hard to see the abundance of money and life. This can result in our wanting to control our lives and our financial situations. Maybe we are afraid to lose out. Maybe we do not sense the caring support that life itself can provide when we open ourselves to it. This support can be experienced through trusting the process of care-based consciousness. You improve your quality of life and that of the planet when you follow the language of your heart.

Let's embrace the concept of overall care and compassion as a starting point for governing our planet. I hope that we can each find our unique contributions, learn to work together, and be in council so we can organize life on our planet accordingly. Let us connect the dots and recognize that love has the power to not just elevate relationships, which is the main realm in which we refer to love, but to elevate and expand all aspects of our culture.

We are not living in illusions when we think of a better world. We see reality; we see a possibility. Let's explore a more beautiful world together, totally grounded in real life; totally grounded in common sense and good business practices, legislation, government policy, and local decision-making. Let's create a beautiful world in which the heart matters.

Chapter 3

Philanthropy for Life – Humanity's True North

Steven Lovink

On Truth, Trust, and Love

Philanthropy for Life's call to action is loud and clear indeed. The guiding energies of the whole of creation embrace this cosmic road map that cherishes the gift of life and compels us to act from a state of true integrity. Combined with the universal principle "as above, so below," it represents a whole-system key or hidden code that can unlock humanity's potential to unleash hidden code to transform finance and unlock humanity's potential to unleash true love for humankind.

This is not unlike resetting our individual and collective compass courses to True North. As long as we experience this True North as *truth* deep in our hearts, we can *trust* and surrender to the knowledge that we will arrive safely at the harbors of our evolutionary destinations while being propelled by *love*. This self-piloting, self-governing, magnetic, and energetically efficient course naturally disentangles our past, present, and future beyond time and space, in the NOW. From this emerges a song of freedom, harmony, and the greater meaning of life. Quite remarkably, we have amazing opportunities to realize the purposes of our lives in unison with realizing the purpose of the whole of life. What a beautiful vision that is!

The same cells of imagination that are found in the gooey, transformational matter inside the chrysalis from which a beautiful butterfly emerges are also hard at work on the fringes of our economic, social, natural, cultural, and spiritual ecosystems. This transformational process signals the creative destruction of habits and belief systems that no longer serve. We often perceive creative "outliers" as lacking potential, and we are only latently conscious of the fact that today's outliers often become tomorrow's leaders. This is in fact how nature's biomimicry works and systems transform. The outliers become leaders and suddenly all universal energy starts self-organizing around a new and better life-sustaining direction that transforms the system as a whole. The transformational process is the manifestation of an evolutionary, creative impulse occurring at extreme points of polarity.

There are examples of such "imaginal" cells at work in subsequent chapters of this book. One could summarize the emergent unified field of love, or "care in action," as a very gooey, experimental mess with promising points of lights, sprouting seeds here and there. But nothing is yet happening at scale, at least not at the scale required to truly transform self and society at the root-cause level. Still, the potential is definitely there. At the cutting and often bleeding edge of this emergent sector we find communities and entrepreneurs who foresee the distinct parts coming together to form the greater whole. It is happening through silent introspection experienced deep within ourselves.

On one end of the spectrum of "desired flow embracing life" we observe an imagining and appreciation of the energetic exchanges that occur in the process of giving and receiving. Let's call it the "art and science of giving and receiving," which is discussed in more detail in part II. This is truly fundamental to the core challenge of reimagining philanthropy. If we either give or receive without consciousness being present; if giving and receiving are not infused with deep care and love; if they are not in "right relationship" (with deep-felt reciprocity, respect, and responsibility), from the local to the global and from the micro to the macro, neither care nor love can bloom, either above or below. (More about right relationship in chapter 15.) It is for this reason that philanthropy must reinvent and align itself on the basis of a cosmic road map that points to True North – in other words, it must embrace the whole of life on a foundation of *truth, trust,* and *love.* It is all about that cosmic flow in harmony with love and life. Philanthropy must flow in ways that unleash true love for humankind.

On the other end of the spectrum of "desired flow embracing life" we find experimentation with redirection of profits in a profit-maximizing commercial world in which human beings have few rights and some privileges, as if the future no longer matters. Do we really understand that not only businesses but also countries, municipalities, church institutions, and all of civil society are in fact organized as corporations that have more (voting) rights than human beings?

We have started to recognize, fortuitously, that our predominantly capitalistic system forces us to choose between money and life, and that unless we somehow infuse our money with the energetic current, resonance, and currency of love, our civilization as we know it is predisposed to die off. We shall remain but a blip on evolution's radar screen, which spans billions of years. Profit-seeking, in unison with philanthropy, must flow to sustain, as opposed to destroy love and life. Our monetary system must become fully aligned with this overarching, life-giving purpose. Without a *biophilic* connection (one that bonds humans to other forms of life), money is just what it is – the emperor without clothes, a fiat currency backed by misguided faith in what does not mirror true wealth: well-being and health for all, sustained by an interconnected planet we all share.

Communities and entrepreneurs exploring the limitless possibilities of reimagining philanthropy in concert with reimagining profits and reimagining money hold the promise and lure of turning a systemic ignition key capable of unleashing true love for humankind. If ever there was a time and a pressing need to find and turn that ignition key, it must be now! So how might we seize the day and accelerate this important process? Let's dive deep.

Life in the Valley of Death

Our human enterprise has entered a "valley of death," a moment of great truth. We find ourselves falling through the cracks of our disintegrating economic, social, natural, cultural, and spiritual foundations as we operate beyond the capacity of many of our planet's resources to sustain our future as a going concern. This capacity has been called our "planetary boundaries," and the level of use of planetary resources that our planet can tolerate has been called the "safe planetary boundaries," by the Stockholm Resilience Centre and author Johan

Rockström.[1] (We use the term *safe planetary boundaries* throughout *Imagining Philanthropy for Life*.) The world around us seems to make less and less sense. Most of us are (and must be) questioning everything. As individual human beings, communities, civil society organizations, businesses, governments, central banks, financial institutions, and gatherings of (poorly) united nations, we feel increasingly impotent. Invariably we experience panic-stricken, frightening free falls into deep abysses of the unknown. Many of us grasp onto branches along the shoreline of a turbulent, even angry river of life. Unless and until we go *with* that flow of life, we will get hurt.

We are descending to the bottom of what reminds me of Otto Sharmer's "Theory U" from which an emergent future becomes visible.[2] This moment of revelation applies to people, groups, organizations, and, in fact, complex adaptive systems everywhere. A growing community of Theory U practitioners now exists, "presencing" the future from this holistic perspective informed from within themselves by open minds, hearts, and wills. Theory U shows how that capacity for presencing can be developed. According to the Presencing Institute's website:

> Presencing is a journey with five movements: As the diagram illustrates, we move down one side of the U (connecting us to the world that is outside our institutional bubble) to the bottom of the U (connecting us to the world that emerges from within) and up the other side of the U (bringing forth the new into the world). On that journey, at the bottom of the U, lies an inner gate that requires us to drop everything that isn't essential. This process of letting-go (of our old ego and self) and letting-come (our highest future possibility: our Self)

establishes a subtle connection to a deeper source of knowing. The essence of presencing is that these two selves — our current self and our best future Self — meet at the bottom of the U and begin to listen and resonate with each other. Once a group crosses this threshold, nothing remains the same. Individual members and the group as a whole begin to operate with a heightened level of energy and sense of future possibility. Often, they then begin to function as an intentional vehicle for an emerging future.[3]

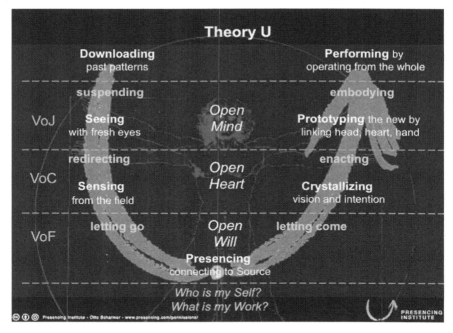

The U Process of Co-sensing and Co-creating – Presencing[3]

The same conundrum often surfaces when someone must choose between realignment with their life purpose and the deceptive comfort of employment with an organization at dissonance with what they hold dear. If they can feel or "presence" into this vulnerable moment with an open mind, an open heart, and a love-inspired will, far-reaching opportunities can arise to crystallize new ways of being and doing. They can embody an intended positive future of the better world we want, bringing forth prototyped microcosms of the possible. These possibilities can then be embedded in well-performing, transformative practices and institutional systems that operate in harmony with the whole of life. Imagine the emergence of an entrepreneurial ecosystem that will bring forth the next Google, Facebook, and breakthrough initiatives that operate in service with the whole of life. Imagine also the relative abundance of micro-, small-, and medium-sized enterprises that serve in harmony with the whole of life.

It is at this very vulnerable pivot point, too, that impactful philanthropic gifts, well-given and well-received, can literally change the world. This is an opportunity to rebalance how we think, act, and transform our relationships to money, love, and life. This new way of being emerges from memories of the aforementioned deep, cosmic pull; and care; and the knowledge that many flowers will bloom. The manifestation of a new reality becomes the mirror of our deepest intentions.

Yet another valley-of-death example concerns our flawed accounting system, which externalizes environmental costs. A recent report by Trucost, sponsored by the United Nations-backed Principles for Responsible Investment and the United Nations Environment Programme Finance Initiative, examined the money earned by the biggest industries on this planet and contrasted it with environmental costs such as water use, land use, greenhouse gas emissions, waste pollution, land pollution, and water pollution.[4] The report found that by taking such unacknowledged costs into effect, none of the industries was actually making a profit. The huge profit margins being made by the world's most profitable industries (oil, meat, tobacco, mining, electronics) are extracted from the future. This means that long-term sustainability is sacrificed for the benefit of shareholders. The report also demonstrated that at times the environmental costs vastly outweighed revenues, implying that these industries would have constantly lost money had they actually been paying for the ecological damage and strain they were causing.

Another way to think about this is that making profits and engaging in philanthropy are funded at the expense of future generations. This contradicts the purported goal of philanthropy as being for the love of humankind. It also reminds us that doing business as usual is myopic and exceedingly short-term-oriented. If we add unacknowledged social costs to this mix, we cannot help but wonder how long the predominant forms of profit-seeking and inside-the-box philanthropy will remain credible pursuits. When we feel or "presence" into this bottom of the U with open minds, hearts, and wills, we can appreciate clearly that any hopeful future must emerge from a life-embracing ecosystem of community and entrepreneurship.

Philanthropy for Life's Proposition

As we weave together the strands of the past, present, and future of philanthropy portrayed in the chapters of this book, we hope you cannot but connect with your heart of hearts with the knowledge that we must breathe life into philanthropy as currently practiced and think outside the boxes of our current belief systems. From these strands a lighthouse emerges that adamantly invites us to reset humanity's compass course to True North – to truth, trust, and love within each and every one of us. This yarn reveals a beautiful keyed code for enhancing the viability of our whole web of life. Palpably visible and felt in the core of our beings, it must also become our song. You are invited to *imagine Philanthropy for Life!*

Let us imagine how Philanthropy for Life can become our song sung as ONE. Consider a self-organizing, cosmically inspired strategy that integrates the ethics of care, represents a whole-system strategy for unleashing true love for humankind, and proposes to:

- *Reframe* our current human-centric experience of philanthropy by activating humanity's resonant alignment with the whole of life.

- *Expand* classical humanistic and social scientific traditions to include the truth that philanthropy in pure form – true love of humankind – can only flourish in harmony with the laws of the universe and nature's wisdom.

- *Engage* all of humanity in embracing Philanthropy for Life as a compass course for maintaining our individual and collective True North based on the truth, trust, and love philanthropy embodies.

- *Embrace* a continuous, lifelong commitment – as opposed to an occasional, casual, or late-in-life commitment – to being fully engaged in philanthropy that is truly *for life* in the here and now.

- *Recognize* that humanity is evolving in harmony with an interconnected universe that creates order out of chaos, enabling higher levels of being and doing propelled by the expansiveness of our individual and collective intentions of love – a reality now clearly established by science, too.

- *Integrate* the original, free, first nations' and first peoples' principles of right relationship – reciprocity, respect, and responsibility – as well-being and health-building blocks for healing their communities, humanity, and the Earth.

- *Activate* the empowerment of individuals and humanity as a whole to become self-sufficient through raising awareness, education, community involvement, and entrepreneurship as the highest forms of energetic giving, and to strategically advance the impacts of philanthropy.

- *Energize* life-sustaining philanthropy through *philanthropreneurship*, which aims to redirect profits to public benefits that resonate with both the greater whole and the common good to effectively address the root causes of humanity's most pressing challenges.

- *Invite* all of humanity, from the local to the global, to transform self and society from within around a shared commitment to the permanence of life on Earth.

Philanthropy for Life's Goals

By imagining Philanthropy for Life as introduced above, a logical and creative foundation for the full expressions of our hearts of hearts is formed that can:

- *Facilitate* synergistic resonance, alignment, cooperation, collaboration, and networking to be catalyzed by a giving circle of conscious "servant-leader" philanthropists to advance Philanthropy for Life.

- *Increase* philanthropic flows to support, honor, and partner with first nations and first peoples as past, current, and future stewards of the whole of life, for, with, on behalf of, and in right relationship with Western culture.

- *Build* capacity for community and entrepreneurship in service with the whole of life, catalyzed by philanthropic gifts and energized by sharing profits for the common good.

- *Integrate* Profits4Life – a voluntary financial mechanism designed to rebalance economic, social, natural, cultural, and spiritual sources and flows in society, thus restoring the very fabric of life. (More about Profits4Life in part III.)

- *Provide* best-of-class venture development, incubation, acceleration, and holistic support services to collaboratively create an emerging ecosystem of community-based, entrepreneurial enterprises in service with the whole of life.

- *Support* the development and implementation of an integrated, collaborative, holographic, online learning and crowdfunding portal that reliably delivers and virally spreads Philanthropy for Life.

- *Bridge* the valleys of death facing communities and entrepreneurs working in service with the whole of life, energized by

Profits4Life and like, complementary, emerging approaches that aim to share profits to regenerate life.

- *Promote* linkages and collaborations with aligned and resonant philanthropists, and motivate investors to advance Philanthropy for Life's ability to succeed beyond our wildest expectations.

- *Influence* and inform fiscal and monetary policies to provide an enabling environment in which Philanthropy for Life can take root, from the local to the global.

- *Stimulate* a growing percentage of total giving to flow to Philanthropy for Life.

- *Set* measurable targets that can be managed and tracked by a family of "Give4Life" indices that advance Philanthropy for Life.

Measuring, Tracking, and Managing Impact

Indices can be developed that communicate how much of our philanthropy flows to life. They would create public awareness about the extent to which we and the world community are committed to navigating safely to our True North destination. Indices function like a well-calibrated compass, conveying truth that we can trust. They also reveal our true love for humankind. Here are some ideas:

- **Give4Life Flow Index:** A series of targets through 2025 could measure, track, and manage flows towards Philanthropy for Life. A back-of-the-envelope calculation shows that if a modest 1 percent of annual giving in the US flowed towards

Philanthropy for Life by 2025 in 0.1 percent annual increments, it could capitalize a fund in excess of $4 billion annually to seed Philanthropy for Life's goals. If *Imagining Philanthropy for Life* is successful at all in making the case for Philanthropy for Life, such a target not only seems reasonable and achievable, but may over time be replaced with more ambitious ones if we consider the sheer scale of humanity's most pressing needs and the potential of raising consciousness.

- **Give4Life Country Index:** The average level of giving has remained stable at 1.9 percent of global GDP over the past 40 years (see "Facts and Figures on Giving" in the next chapter). This particular index would measure and track targets for overall generosity set through 2025 on a country-by-country basis, and make visible what portion of giving flows to Philanthropy for Life and how corporations, foundations, governments, civil society organizations, and individuals each play active roles.

- **Give4Life Profitability Index:** US corporate pre-tax profits in 2013 were at 12.5 percent, their highest level in at least 85 years; employee compensation was at the lowest level in 65 years; top CEOs make 300 times more than typical workers; corporate giving represents 5 percent of total giving.[5] This index would highlight companies' profitability and total corporate giving, including flows to Philanthropy for Life.

- **Give4Life Reciprocity Index:** Less than 1 percent of total giving flows to first nations and first peoples worldwide, yet they are the most effective stewards of Earth.[6] This index would set targets through 2025 for increasing flows of giving to their communities and causes, communicating and expressing our collective responsibility, respect, and desire to be in right relationship with them as equals on a planet we all share and to honor future generations.

- **Give4Life Financial Index:** The banking and finance sector has been capturing a growing, destabilizing portion of worldwide GDP. It has created massive amounts of wealth for a small segment of the world population at the expense of life. Its licenses to operate responsibly as services to humankind might need to be revoked or at least fundamentally reconsidered. A starting point could be a measure that would ensure that its ability to create money out of nothing and place bets in the global "casino" is at least systemically linked to a commitment to Philanthropy for Life. Modest, global, Give4Life "life-insurance" transaction fees on trading stocks, bonds, and currencies; creating money through debt; and other international financial transactions could instantaneously unlock very large flows of financial resources. They could finance an integrated ecosystem that operates in service with the whole of life, catalyzed by philanthropic giving for life.

- **Give4Life Love Index:** If we measure Philanthropy for Life in monetary terms alone, we miss the point of the love-based economy that exists largely outside of the confining box of our monetary systems. A Give4Life Love Index would track volunteer services of time, talent, and creativity committed to our communities, our families, and ourselves for sustaining well-being and health. Volunteerism is a tradition that made America great when it was founded and it was necessary to "raise that barn" in the absence of adequate money for financing our early pioneering efforts.

- **Give4Life Matching Index:** Matched funding constructions are effective ways to engage and leverage Philanthropy for Life flows from different sectors of society. For example, a modest percentage of government, business, and civil society organization budgets could match giving by the general public to crowdfund what we want to manifest through Philanthropy for Life. We can set targets and track and manage them.

Humanity's True North?

At this point you may need to suspend judgement as to whether Philanthropy for Life will be humanity's True North. Philanthropy for Life's core proposition, goals, and metrics may not yet be sufficiently clear without the added benefit of an exploration of philanthropy's past, present, and future, as well as a series of inspiring stories of transformation of self and society that exemplify the importance of embracing the whole of life. Together they represent the foundational *raison d'être* for Philanthropy for Life. It is these contextual building blocks, elucidating urgency and need, to which we turn next.

PART II

Exploring Philanthropy's Past, Present, and Future

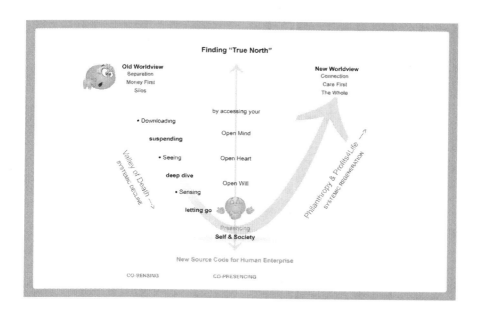

Chapter 4

True Love for Humankind through Time and Space

Steven Lovink

What Is Philanthropy?

We do not always seem to have a clear understanding of what is meant by philanthropy. Before we endeavor to reimagine philanthropy by thinking outside the box, it is helpful to first explore what we mean by philanthropy and how it is typically defined.

The search term "philanthropy" on Google.com provides us with the following description:

> the desire to promote the welfare of others, expressed especially by the generous donation of money to good causes

synonyms: benevolence, generosity, humanitarianism, public-spiritedness, altruism, social conscience, charity, charitableness, brotherly love, fellow feeling, magnanimity, munificence, liberality, largesse, openhandedness, bountifulness, beneficence, unselfishness, humanity, kindness, kindheartedness, compassion; historical almsgiving "a family noted for its philanthropy"

North American: a philanthropic institution; a charity

At Merriam-Webster.com, straightforward and full definitions are provided as follows:

Simple: The practice of giving money and time to help make life better for other people.

Full: Goodwill to fellow members of the human race; especially: active effort to promote human welfare; an act or gift done or made for humanitarian purposes; an organization distributing or supported by funds set aside for humanitarian purposes.

Catalogue for Philanthropy sees philanthropy's definition as interacting with both long-standing classical, humanistic, cultural roots and the now-dominating social scientific culture that emerged in the twentieth century. The organization advocates a balanced approach between these two cultural perspectives and believes philanthropy is best defined as:

private initiatives for public good (the social-science aspect) focusing on quality of life (the humanistic aspect).

This definition neatly distinguishes private initiatives from initiatives by "government (public initiatives for public good) and business (private initiatives for private good)."[1]

Apart from the definitional subtleties surrounding understandings of philanthropy, such as whether charitable giving is the same as philanthropy or vice versa (which is addressed later herein), there is the core identity question: Who is a philanthropist? A frequent misconception typifies philanthropy as acts of generous giving that most rich and famous people are known for. Such is often the case, but the perception and practice of what it means to be a philanthropist are shifting rapidly.

For the purpose of *Imagining Philanthropy for Life*, its authors consider every responsible global citizen and sovereign human being to be a potential philanthropist through direct and indirect acts of giving money, time, talent, kindness, and possessions to the cause(s) of their choice. We are also mindful that philanthropy is not and has never been only about money. Before arriving at any premature conclusions about these definitional issues and who is or is not a philanthropist and why, let us travel through time and space for added perspective.

On Promethean Fire and Hope

Few of us can avoid being fascinated with the mystery of life at the point of conception, be it the birth of the universe, the stars, Earth, humanity, plants, animals, ourselves, life's DNA, or even the proverbial grain of sand on the beach, which contains the composition of a whole universe of life's design mirroring things "as above, so below." The big questions such as Where do I/we come from? Why am I / are we here? What is my/our purpose? and How can I/we contribute to the world? are alive and well in most of us.

We often deeply intuit but too quickly forget that the whole of life must be appreciated as one big gift. Bang! There it was, a bountiful present, out of nowhere and born in love, to be received in gratitude – a life-giving, abundant endowment propelled by a caring yet disciplined universe to be cherished, cared for, and nurtured not only for our lifetimes but for generations to come. For with selfless giving comes the spiritual responsibility to receive with grace, symbolizing the deeply entangled, meaningful right relationship that reflects the art and science of giving and receiving.

This Big Bang of a gift bestowed upon us may well be described as philanthropic in nature, in the sense that it was offered to us via mysterious, cosmic intervention for the love of humankind. It offered (and always does in every instance) the free choice of each and every human being to become a philanthropist. Let's explore and unpack why this is so.

Our voyage through time and space starts with the archetypical, mythical story of the titan Prometheus, who stole fire from the heavens to light up (the DNA of) struggling humans with optimism and hope. It is in the circa 460 BCE Greek play *Prometheus Bound*, attributed to the playwright Aeschylus, that we find the first recorded use of the term *philanthropy*.[2] The word comes from the Greek *phil* = love, and *anthropos* = man, which translates to "for the love of man," or perhaps better, "for the love of humankind." The play tells the story of Prometheus who, having molded humans from clay, was not satisfied with his creations. Prometheus's frustration was that humanity was not yet endowed with culture such as the arts, sciences, technology, knowledge, and skills – in other words, humans were unable to become civilized. Prometheus felt that humans dwelled fearfully in dark caves and could not live up to their full potential or what it means to be human. Zeus, the almighty tyrannical ruler of the universe, even wanted to annihilate Prometheus's sorry clay innovations.

Instead, the "humanity-loving character" of the rebellious Prometheus sparked, as it were, humanity's further evolution with the gift of fire (the arts, sciences, technology, knowledge, and essential life skills) and the characteristics of optimism and hope – all stolen from the heavens. Prometheus's vision was that there would be no future for humanity without hope and optimism, nor would there be a future without fire.

It was an intervention with "foresight" (the meaning of Prometheus's name), designed to improve the human condition (the "public good or purpose") with support from his mother, Gaia (Earth). Prometheus's entrepreneurial spirit and independence brought upon this great benefactor of humanity the wrath of Zeus, for which he would suffer eternally. *Prometheus Bound* played to the sentiments of Greeks and Romans interested in the nature and origin of civilization, which the play attributed to a mythic "love of what it is to be human." By endowing humanity with this attribute, Prometheus was essentially completing not only *his* creation, but also that of humanity, including the capacity for humans to be philanthropic themselves.

The philosophical dictionary of Plato's Academy, founded in 387 BCE by a group working for the public good on a volunteer basis, listed *philanthropía* as:

A state of well-educated habits, stemming from love of humanity. A state of being productive of benefit to humans. A state of grace. Mindfulness together with good works.[3]

Generosity across World Traditions

The archetypical story of Prometheus describes a human condition remarkably reminiscent of the slowly evolving way of life throughout several hundreds of thousands of years of our human prehistory – a time when we indeed lived in caves and before we quite suddenly acquired the knowledge to grow food from seeds, make wine and beer, and use more advanced tools; a time way before the early Mesopotamia, Indus Valley, ancient Egypt, Maya, China, ancient Greek, Persia, Rome, Inca, and Aztec civilizations emerged. It was a time, too, after which the monetary system and its connection to gold appeared in Sumer, and "first creation" was described on Sumerian tablets (circa 6,000 BCE).

While the impulse for philanthropy has deep, common roots in Western human history and mythology, we can find elements of the gift of Promethean fire and hope in creation stories across our major world traditions. Without fail, generosity, giving, and charity were always valued as good, generative acts of kindness that benefitted the whole of society as well as self. They are invariably considered internalized parts of a deeply fulfilling, actualized, responsible human life path. Even when considering the less-well-known speculated prehistory of the lost civilizations of Lemuria and Atlantis, societal virtues and values of charitable giving appear to have been known, practiced, and honored. They have found their way via symbols, artifacts, and shared but differentiated creation mythologies into diverse cultures of far-flung peoples across the globe in known historical times, including having been embedded in the eventual belief systems of our world's major faiths.

In Eastern traditions, for example:

Hinduism has since times memorial been inspired by the ancient texts of the Upanishads (1,000 – 500 BC). From the *Bhagavad Gita* we learn that "Charity which is given without consideration of anything in return, at a sanctified and holy place and at an astrologically auspicious time, given as a matter of duty to one qualified; that charity is regarded as the nature of goodness."[4]

Buddhism is well known for valuing generosity and service to others as vital; it is an essential practice on the path to enlightenment. Buddhism considers one to coexist in a vast web of life, continuously receiving the generosity of other people. We can choose to develop loving kindness by learning to give in all ways to all beings. The Buddha (566 – 486 BCE) said, "If you knew what I know about the power of giving, you would not let a single meal pass without sharing it in some way."[5]

Islamism deeply values charity as well; it is an integral part of what it means to be a good Muslim.

Confucianism considers charitable giving in the context of benevolence (*ren*) and righteousness (*yi*) as described in the book of Mencius (372 – 289 BCE), where "*ren* is the heart, *yi* is the path." Likewise, giving (*shi*) is to act for the sake of others for whom the generous heart has compassion, and its meaning is linked to the idea of *shu*, which is a reciprocal relationship between oneself and another. A broader sense of *shu* represents the notion that giving is an enabling act for helping others stand on their own feet.

This concept of giving that empowers one to stand on their own feet through education, imparting skills, or helping someone set up a business was codified circa 1,180 CE by Maimonides in Jewish law. It is considered the highest level of giving. How giving relates to community and entrepreneurship in service with the whole of life will be explored in more detail in later chapters of this book.

The first peoples exploring the Earth for hundreds of thousands of years before modern times survived by embracing principles of reciprocity, respect, and responsibility – right relationship – as we will discover. Tithing, a form of mandatory tax to help the poor, is an ancient Hebrew practice dating back to 2,500 BCE. Roman civilization, inspired by Greek thought, adopted philanthropic pursuits such as those exemplified by the first Roman emperor Augustus in 28 BCE, who was known for providing public aid to several hundred thousand of his people. Julius Caesar initiated the coining of his currency to advance good works (think fire and hope), but not unlike Prometheus, may well have paid the ultimate price.

Numerous additional examples can be provided as testimony of a timeless story that tells us that charity, giving, kindness, and generosity for the love of humankind – its shadow sides included – genuinely reside within our psyches, beliefs, and value systems. Promethean philanthropy's archetype is mirrored across world traditions, time, and space. It is fused into the DNA of our shared human history, our *karma*, our *dharma*, and our innate, now scientifically proven, wired inclination towards altruism.

In the Greek tradition, philanthropy was often linked to freedom (Prometheus's rebellious action) and democracy (fire and hope). It became the seed of an idea that would later catch fire and hope during the American Revolution.

Philanthropy in the New World

Different perspectives reveal both bright and shadowy sides of philanthropy's evolution at the time of the discovery of the New World, and since. After the fall of the Roman Empire in 500 CE, much of Western civilization plunged into the Dark Ages, and the traditional understanding of philanthropy remained mostly forgotten on the shelves of medieval monastic libraries for over a thousand years. Then came an era during which the emerging trinity of church, state, and the merchant banking class collaborated to redraw the map of a yet to be fully discovered and conquered world, including the Americas!

Not until 1608 would the word *philanthropia* surface in the English language in an essay called "On Goodness" by Sir Francis Bacon, and in 1623 *philanthropie* was used synonymously with *humanitie* in a first English dictionary written by Sir Henry Cockeram. It was at that same time that on the wings of the Enlightenment in Europe the traditional ideas and values of philanthropy found their way to what would become the United States of America. These inspired many of the Founding Fathers, and a culture of collaboration and voluntary associations took on numerous projects for public good.

In *Philanthropy Reconsidered*, written by George McCully in 2008, we learn that the United States of America was conceived and dedicated as a philanthropic nation – a gift to all humankind – to enhance the human condition through freedom and democracy. It symbolized "a new 'fire,' inspired with a new 'blind hope' – squarely in the Promethean tradition." George Washington was a philanthropist and volunteer. He signed many of his letters "Philanthropically yours." In 1935 Alexis de Tocqueville published *Democracy in America*, in which he highlighted the philanthropic spirit of America as one of the country's key strengths.[6]

The shadow side of the discovery of the New World still harbors the long overdue truth, reconciliation, and healing of the entire world's history of colonization, slavery, and treatment of first peoples. It is related to the ripple effects of Papal Bulls issued in 1493 and 1496, the doctrines of which were carried forward into US law as the Doctrine of Discovery.[7] If ever there was an opportunity for a twenty-first century philanthropic initiative addressing the root causes of the world's suffering and societal ills, we would dare to hold our entangled past, present, and future in the light of what we can do now to change that reality.

The Nineteenth and Twentieth Centuries

During the nineteenth century the classical ideas and values of philanthropy became less and less influential as the Industrial Revolution gathered steam. By the beginning of the twentieth century great fortunes had been amassed by the titans of industry. It was a time when Carnegie, Ford, Rockefeller, and others established their private foundations.

From that point forward philanthropy became a more strategic, professional, sophisticated, and socially engineered practice. The US Congress passed the Revenue Act in 1913, exempting charitable organizations from paying taxes, which spurred their growth. Corporations were allowed to deduct charitable contributions as of 1935. Philanthropy became increasingly focused on group behavior, and charitable giving began to address root causes of societal ills as opposed to symptoms. Society became viewed as consisting of government, business, and civil society sectors that could be strategically managed to deliver socially engineered results. Relationships with individual donors, recipients, and volunteers became more distant and abstract.

The now large nonprofit sector in the US became large only during the last quarter of the twentieth century. The term *nonprofit* originated with the IRS and refers to the entire civil society sector, including charities. There are now well over a million nonprofit organizations in the US, but only 16 percent of charitable contributions are truly philanthropic in nature.[8]

Charity is about giving to people and causes that have urgent, immediate needs and short-term objectives. Philanthropy is meant to address root causes and long-term objectives. We need to ask ourselves whether it might not be better to increase our philanthropic giving in order to help prevent crises from happening in the first place. Our generosity should take the long view by focusing on the permanence of life, thereby diminishing the very need for charity.

Twenty-First-Century Philanthropy

Our current century has seen the emergence of a wave of reimagined forms of philanthropy including venture philanthropy, philanthrocapitalism, philanthropreneurship, conscious philanthropy, effective philanthropy, strategic philanthropy, integrated philanthropy, grassroots philanthropy, kids' philanthropy, and more. Emerging solutions and trends will be addressed in more detail in a subsequent chapter, but three significant ones are highlighted below.

The Giving Pledge, launched in 2010 by Bill and Melinda Gates, invites wealthy individuals and their families in America and throughout the world to dedicate the majority of their wealth to philanthropy. It is an effort to help address society's most pressing problems by inviting the world's wealthiest individuals and families to commit to giving more than half of their wealth to philanthropic or charitable causes either during their lifetimes or in their wills. It is a moral and not a legal obligation. The pledge encourages signatories to find their unique ways to give that inspire them personally and benefit society. As of this writing almost 200 billionaires have signed up, signaling that $30+ trillion in philanthropic flows will be infused into root causes around the world.[9]

Wealthy individuals and their families not only recognize the need to be actively engaged with philanthropic efforts, but also to commit to be being so earlier in life and to give away ever-greater percentages of their wealth. This is important because it circulates money back into society sooner and in larger amounts. These funds can address root causes of societal ills. For example, Facebook founder Mark Zuckerberg, who is 33 as I write this, has committed to giving away 99 percent of his fortune, which is pegged at some $45 billion and still growing.

Another trend is the growing interest of celebrities from sports, movies, music, and other fields to set up foundations and donate to their favorite causes. Many of them start young, so they serve as encouraging role models for the next generation of philanthropists, small, medium, and large.

Important to reflect on is that significant differences in philanthropic impact result from giving (back) at the end of one's life versus during one's life; or better yet, giving forward now. The earlier money recirculates, the better.

Facts and Figures on Giving

What does the current philanthropic landscape look like by the numbers? The US can be considered a generous nation when compared to the rest of the world. The Charities Aid Foundation (CAF) World Giving Index rates the US as the second-most-generous nation after tiny Myanmar, followed by New Zealand, Canada, and Australia. China ranks among the five least generous countries. This lack of generosity appears to be due to a still-nascent nonprofit sector combined with a weak tax incentive structure. And we should remember that giving money is but one measure of generosity. Philanthropy should not be defined by money flows alone. The World Giving Index, for example, measures the percentage of people in each country who donate money, volunteer, or help a stranger. One hundred forty-five countries were surveyed in 2015, representing about 96 percent of the world's population. In 2015, 2.2 billion people helped a stranger, 1.4 billion donated money, and 1 billion volunteered.[10]

From Giving USA's 2015 Annual Report (reflecting 2014 figures) we learn the following:[11]

- Most Americans give to charity (95.4%) at an average of $2,950 per family. A slightly larger percentage of the wealthy (98.4%) give, averaging $65,580 per gift. Mega-gifts from high-net-worth individuals (HNWIs) of $2 million and higher have been on the rise, lifting overall average giving levels. People who do not make a lot of money are as generous as a percentage of their incomes as the very wealthy. All in all, charitable contributions in 2014 reached an average of $1,050 per person in the US, the equivalent of $358 billion for the nation as a whole.

- Contributions came predominantly from individuals (72% or $258 billion) followed by foundations (15% or $54 billion), bequests (8% or $28 billion), and last, corporations (5% or $18 billion). Contributions were allocated to leading causes of 10 recipient categories: religion (32% or $115 billion), education (15% or $55 billion), human services (12% or $42 billion), gifts to foundations (12% or $42 billion), health (8% or $30 billion), public society benefit (7% or $26 billion), art/culture/humanities (5% or $17 billion), international affairs (4% or $15 billion), environment/animals (3% or 10 billion), and individuals (2% or $7 billion).

- A growing portion of Americans is giving online, accounting for 6.7 percent of fundraising in 2014, with several funding platforms reporting as much as $45 million in processed gifts. While online giving is still a modest percentage of total giving, it is accelerating rapidly (8.9% in 2014), and its share of total giving is expected to continue an accelerating upward trend.

And from various sources:

- A fact deserving close attention is that while US giving since the early 1970s has been growing more or less in tune with the overall health of the economy in absolute terms, charitable contributions as a percentage of GDP have remained stuck at an average of 2 percent of US GDP.[12,13] This phenomenon is related to historically extreme levels of income and wealth inequality. America's rating, compared to other nations, on the relationship between income equality and an index of health and social problems, is quite sobering. The underlying reason is that corporate profit margins have risen to a recent 40-year high of 12.5 percent, while labor's share of income declined to 40-year lows and salaries of S&P 500 CEOs now average 375 times that of the average worker.[14,15]

- The ability of 95 percent or more of the population of the US to give money has necessarily diminished because their share of total income and wealth has been eroding over time. It is the mega-gifts from HNWIs earning $2 million and more that have grown in number. Together with a relatively more generous percentage of charitable donations given by people with income levels below $75,000, charitable donations have remained stable at 2 percent of global GDP. We must ask ourselves whether this situation is sustainable. Many a thought leader would argue that we are dancing on the precipice of a collapse of our financial system as we know it. If capitalism in its present form no longer works for the whole of society, what other options can we consider?

For Reflection and Dialogue

A genuine potential of philanthropy's ability to transform self and society is yet to be realized. It will become the gift to humanity that has been hidden in plain sight. Many are familiar with the story of the shoe salesperson who was sent on a mission by his boss to explore new opportunities on the continent of Africa. The salesperson returned profoundly disappointed after months of arduous travel, trials, and tribulations. *Imagine,* he was worriedly thinking, *few people wear shoes, nobody wants shoes, there is no market for shoes.* With trepidation he reported back to his entrepreneurial boss and explained his assessment of the African market for shoes. A few days later the boss and the salesperson, with his belief system turned upside down by his boss, were back on an airplane to Africa, and what an enormous untapped market for shoes they opened!

A similar story may one day be told of the world's market opportunity for philanthropy. Can we imagine philanthropy gaining a much larger percentage of GDP when we must also consider that philanthropy (giving) and profit (taking) are competing for capital from opposing ends of the financial-market continuum? Suffice it to say that the need for philanthropy (market opportunity) is great. When we consider basic human needs in Africa, in developing countries, in inner US cities, and in Native American and US veteran communities, and the increasing concentration of wealth and its flip side – poverty, there is no lack of reasons to grow our philanthropic efforts into a much larger and impactful share of our GDP. The same can be said about the need and urgency of maintaining our ecosystems, which are our sources of water, clean energy, health, food, and biodiversity sustaining the whole of humanity.

There are three fundamental questions we must ask ourselves:

1. If 98 percent of US GDP (which grows with war, disease, disasters, and externalized costs of business as usual) is not philanthropic – that is, not necessarily purposed for the love of humankind in harmony with nature – what does this predict about our quality of life in the future?

2. If only 2 percent of US GDP is directed to philanthropic activities, how can the direction of these funding flows be leveraged to transform the composition of 98 percent of our GDP towards a true love of humankind?

3. Can you think of three ways each to (a) increase your charitable contributions (time, money, etc.) towards your own life and your family life, and (b) increase your generous contributions (time, money, etc.) to the root causes of the pressing societal challenges we face?

Chapter 5

Challenges Facing the Art and Science of Giving

Steven Lovink

On True North

We live in a spinning, fast-changing, and interconnected world. More than ever before we need to keep our internal compasses pointed to True North to guide us successfully through life. Adhering to True North maintains our authenticity, helps us achieve the purposes of our lives and further those of our organizations, and assists us in realizing our fullest potential. The same holds true for the human enterprise as a whole. It has become a challenge for us to operate within safe planetary boundaries, from the local to the global. We strive to sustain resilient social, cultural, and spiritual relations and thrive by means of responsible economic and financial systems. Our systems require redesign to function in service with that True North.

Governments, businesses, civil society organizations, and citizens everywhere share an interdependent responsibility to collaborate effectively towards this harmonizing, unifying goal. On this collective journey into consciousness it is important to keep track of our bearings, because even the smallest deviation results in ending up in quite a different place. If we consider our fraying web of economic, social, natural, cultural, and spiritual life, it is safe to state that we are already way off course. Our philanthropy – our love of humanity – is challenged to seize its unique potential to become the galvanizing force for good and inspire system-wide transformational change – a role other societal actors cannot or will not perform. But are our philanthropic efforts pointed to True North?

Big Issues and Questions

Inside the box of US institutionalized philanthropy, which represents 15 percent of giving, the big issues according to the Center for Effective Philanthropy's (CEP) president, Phil Buchanan, can be liberally summarized as follows:[1]

1. Philanthropy is often perceived to be part of the so-called establishment, which suffers from eroded public trust precipitated by the banking crisis, the dysfunctional Congress, a less-than-democratic process aggravated by the "Citizens United" ruling, and mounting social unrest and activism in response to each of these. As US institutions and "the establishment" are challenged, courage is required for foundations to more fully align their program goals and priorities to address root causes of humanity's most pressing problems, such as influencing the

status quo through policy initiatives, addressing social and racial inequalities, reinforcing food systems and security, and combating climate change. These efforts need to be community driven as opposed to being driven by private funding for public goods for private interests. In today's context, donor-driven top-down approaches are no longer efficient or acceptable. Most of all, foundations need to have their ears to the ground and listen for the systemic issues that matter most to society, and then align and take action within that dynamic flow in cooperation with others.

2. Large philanthropic endowments are typically managed to realize an endless time horizon, with 95 percent of US endowments invested to maximize returns, leaving only 5 percent for program-related investments. The practice of *negative screening* to prevent money from flowing to socially irresponsible industries and corporate practices is still relatively rare, represented by 17 percent of total funds. The above implies that foundations often seek to preserve their capital by investing in a status quo that furthers a long list of societal ills, contradicting their own purported philanthropic missions.

There are exceptions, and change is on the way. Atlantic Philanthropies is in the final stages of spending itself out of existence. McKnight Foundation committed to investing 10 percent of its endowment in alignment with its mission. F. B. Heron Foundation spends all of its endowment on *impact investments* – investments having greater impacts on beneficial change than traditional investments – that address systemic societal ills, and challenges its peers to do the same. The Rockefeller Brothers Fund decided to divest from fossil fuels along with now some 150–200 foundations following its example. Others such as Coca-Cola, Nestle, and General Electric pursue Michael Porter's concept of "shared value," doing social good and making a profit; but we should be mindful that the credibility of such an approach depends on the intrinsic nature or goodness of the business.

3. Good philanthropic strategy and its measurement are never easy. Foundations have always cared deeply about effectiveness and impact. Advances in social science and behavioral approaches tested by the first big mega-foundations that were established in the early 1900s exemplified this caring approach.

In the 1990s and 2000s business schools taught that foundations need to emphasize their unique value. But what works in a competitive business context does not necessarily work in a real-world philanthropic context in which impact rather than profit must be the primary goal. Social returns on investment are hard to measure and quantify; assessing the performance of foundations is relatively easier, yet remains highly contextual and is still complex. The transparency of foundations' workings, however, could be much enhanced. There is also a need to support nonprofit organizations in gathering necessary data in order to make these determinations. Foundation boards thus need to work with staff to define meaningful indicators for gauging progress, and learn from the data to pierce what has been dubbed a comfortable "bubble of positivity" by CEP's Phil Buchanan.

4. A collaborative effort among philanthropic foundations or, in Buchanan's words, "the embracing of – or return to – aligned action among funders (and with other actors)," presents another challenge for achieving impact. Unlike the pursuit of a business mission to earn profit based on proprietary know-how, technology, and quick capture of market share, tackling the systemic, societal root causes of humanity's most pressing problems at the required scale is a doomed strategy unless it is pursued with others.

   Such endeavors need to reach beyond expressing mere interest in collaboration and paying lip service to the idea. They need to reflect a real commitment to one unified goal while parking personal as well as organizational egos at the door. Achieving tangible impact is about "servant leadership" – leadership born of the will to serve rather than to exert power – combined with "servant followship" in supporting those who know best what they are doing. It also embraces a shared, bigger, and uplifting vision of how to serve the greater philanthropic mission beyond limiting parochial interests.

5. Nonprofits are more than just implementing agencies, contractors, and vendors that execute the grant programs of foundations; nonprofits need to be enabled in more sophisticated ways to become more impactful. Grantors

and grantees need to be in right relationship with aligned partners working on a shared mission, informed by a shared vision, and based on shared underlying values that cement the alliance's impact. The impacts that nonprofits have are known to correlate with the amount of general operating support they receive for growing their organizations. Confining overheads to an average of 20 – 25 percent of grant dollars is often shortsighted; it condemns foundations and nonprofits to thinking small. The business world has much more flexibility for optimizing, aligning, and financing the costs of running their operations for impact and success.

Perceptions are changing. An increasing number of large foundations is now committed to rules governing overheads that allow for higher proportions of grant dollars for overheads. Managing overheads remains relevant, such as in the case of for-profit fundraisers that keep 50–75 percent of dollars raised. But perpetuating the overhead myth is a disservice to achieving impact. Nonprofits need to be listened to, and foundations need to think outside the still-current box.

The Love Economy

Outside the box of the world of philanthropic foundations and corporations – in philanthropy by and for people, which represents 72 percent of giving in the US – there are challenges. Such philanthropy can be thought of as generous acts of loving kindness towards humanity and ourselves, in other words philanthropy that gives to self and society for the love of humankind.

If you are like most people, you probably don't consider yourself a philanthropist. Philanthropy is for the very wealthy and famous, right? But let me invite you on a little journey with me that might well shift your perspective, as it has mine. The truth is most everyone can be a philanthropist. The barrier to overcome is one of genuine commitment.

Philanthropy is often thought of as giving money, but this a limiting belief. We can also give of our time, expertise, knowledge, possessions, or even positive thoughts – they represent what Hazel Henderson called The Love Economy. Of these, time is perhaps the most precious, as we have only so much of it on a daily basis and during our lifetimes.

There are 24 hours in a day, seven days in a week, and 52 weeks in a year. Most adults need about eight hours of sleep a day, work eight hours a day (depending on their culture), and have another eight hours available for elective activities to nourish themselves and others, such as family, schooling, home responsibilities, sports, hobbies, community service, faith, volunteering, and extra work, with an extra 16 hours available for these elective activities on weekends. To this we can typically add two to six weeks of vacation time and public holidays, depending on where you live in the world. We now have a bird's-eye view of a typical time budget; we can imagine how a portion of this budget can be allocated to charitable purposes and what the tradeoffs between sleeping, working, and recreational hours might be in a day to make a difference.

The saying goes that charity should always start by being charitable to oneself and should not be limited to others. Charity towards oneself makes much sense, for how can we be charitable to others, even close family, if we have not taken care of our basic needs first?

These needs start with sleep. A good night's rest enables and sustains the self-healing processes in our bodies and minds. Sleep is regenerative, and without it, or by accumulating a sleep deficit as many of us do, we deprive ourselves of the ability to be fit, rested, alert, and at the top of our games during waking hours. Chronic lack of sleep, whatever its causes, undermines one's health, is tantamount to not being charitable to oneself, and ultimately affects one's ability to be charitable to others. Better is to get sufficient sleep. It is a life-sustaining form of philanthropy benefitting self, loved ones, and society as a whole.

What we do with our time during waking hours is equally relevant to our abilities to be generous to self and society. First and foremost, we should again consider our health, which along with the quality of our sleep is profoundly affected by a healthy diet and sufficient exercise. To the extent that our food is healthy and we remain fit and resilient through regular exercise, our productivity and creativity are enhanced, making us better parents, better students, more valuable workers and entrepreneurs, and potentially more generous philanthropists.

Health statistics on sleep, diet, and exercise are often sobering and tend to show that on the whole modern humans would benefit from more sleep, healthier foods, and greater exercise. These statistics suggest that much of the world's population is not compassionate with self and that the prospects for charitable or philanthropic giving to society are impaired and could be improved. Perhaps in part because of this lack of well-being, health is the top cause for philanthropic giving throughout the world. One cannot but wonder how much of this charitable giving is targeted at primary sleep, nutrition, and exercise programs that could potentially sustain everyone's health, resilience, and ability to be philanthropic.

Beyond attaining sufficient sleep, diet, and exercise, which are essential prerequisites of being fit enough to be generous philanthropists, we must be able to provide for our families and loved ones within the economic and financial systems of our working lives.

These systems need to work in harmony within our safe planetary boundaries and provide sufficiently robust social foundations. It is in this realm that the whole of humanity is not performing very responsibly. Nature's way and those of most people exhibit an innate drive to be sustainable, self-sufficient, and resilient, and to flourish. Nature has been evolving successfully over 3.8 billion years, while humans made a relatively recent appearance on Earth some 2.5 million years ago. Nature will continue to successfully innovate, adapt, grow, survive, and flourish despite our efforts to deplete much of Earth's resources and her ability to regenerate. The case for humanity is less clear. Humans may well remain but a blip on the radar screen of universal history unless they embrace living in harmony with nature and the tried, underlying laws of the universe. After all, everything is interconnected and one.

On Giving, Receiving, and Altruism

During the acts of giving and receiving, a sort of magic happens. Altruism, the selfless concern for the benefit of others, is said to be wired deep within us and appears to serve a distinct evolutionary purpose. It is a form of exchange in which parts coming together create a greater whole. Our altruism, giving, and receiving also make us feel good, reduce stress, and release dopamine, serotonin, and oxytocin, which can even be addictive. One could say that there is an art and science to giving and receiving – and to altruism, which is fundamentally about individual and group well-being and creating something together from love.

This dynamic, relational balance or wholeness should be honored from within, yet it is frequently abandoned, forgotten, or lost during the exchange of giving and receiving. We have already seen that throughout the ages philanthropy and charitable giving have played significant roles across all world traditions. Ancient wisdom conveys to us that giving is more generative, satisfying, honorable, healthy, liberating, and happy than taking. Humanity has been taking more of the gift of life than it has been giving back. The circular flow of life is interrupted when we consistently take more than we give, even if we try to compensate for it later in life when we feel wealthy and secure.

And so it is that current and future generations inherit a planet and peoples who are depleted, damaged, and in need of regeneration. We are fortunately increasingly aware that time is of the essence in transforming our local operating systems into a global one. I believe philanthropy has a significant role to play in precipitating positive system-wide transformation, but it must first recalibrate its moral compass to avoid losing its very soul and purpose. For when we give – as in prevailing approaches to public, private, and corporate philanthropic giving, such giving perpetuates a dependency culture and *quid-pro-quo* relationships, be they by design or the result of unintended consequences.

We can give of our generosity in many ways. Maimonides (1135-1204) was the great codifier of Jewish law who formulated a list of eight levels of giving, which he called "doing justice," that pertain to giving money and all other forms of giving. These levels correlate to the degree to which the giver is sensitive to the needs and feelings of the recipient(s), and to the nature of the relationship:

- The lowest or eighth level of giving is to give grudgingly, with a sour disposition. It comes from a sense of guilt or obligation as opposed to care and love.

- The seventh level is to give less than you can afford but to do so in a nice way that is a sincere expression of interest and empathy to help someone along, although it does not fully meet the recipient's entire need.

- The sixth level involves giving generously, but only when asked. The giver addresses the need of a recipient genuinely and is aware of how difficult it may have been for the recipient to call for help.

- The fifth level is giving proactively, before being asked. The giver demonstrates sensitivity and anticipates and seeks out opportunities to make a difference.

- Level four is when the recipient knows the giver, but not the reverse. In this case the giver is humble, yet the recipient still feels shame and inferiority, for they know their benefactor.

- The third level is the opposite of level four. It is when the giver knows the recipient, but not the reverse. It preserves the dignity of the recipient because the donation is anonymous, but the donor can still feel a sense of superiority or dominance.

- The second level of giving is when one gives anonymously, and giver and recipient do not know each other. It is to be implemented via a trusted, honest, and discreet intermediary (charitable organization) on a voluntary basis, allows egos to merge and dissolve, and prevents one person feeling inferior or superior to the other.

- The first and highest level of giving is helping someone become self-sufficient. The giver helps others get a job, learn new skills, set up a business, or form a partnership, for example. This level of giving is empowering, builds the confidence of the recipient, and addresses basic human needs to feel needed and capable. The relationship puts the recipient in a position in which they can contribute philanthropically to the community as well.[2]

Applying the above wisdom to giving and receiving mirrors timeless lessons of self-reflection in regard to our charitable works. Most world traditions emphasize the importance of the quality of exchange between donor and recipient. Somehow we seem to have forgotten much of this wisdom, but fortunately we can rediscover its lasting truth.

For philanthropy to address the love of humankind systemically for the long term, it must not only empower, partner with, and enable humanity to fish, but also reach beyond to consider the interconnectivity of the whole supply chain from fish to market and beyond.

Charity versus Philanthropy

A frequently asked question concerns the differences between charity and philanthropy and to what extent they are alike. They are alike in that practitioners of philanthropy and charity have the same motivation: they share a sense of compassion and they want to give generously of themselves to help others. Both charity and philanthropy have the intended effect of uplifting people, communities, countries – even the world; but they reach desired outcomes differently. Related are the frequently asked questions of how we can best help the poor, whether that is through charity or philanthropy, and how it is enabling as opposed to creating relationships based on dependency.

The differences are that charity has a shorter term, small-world focus, and aims to address immediate needs as a result of a deep sense or understanding of the suffering and misery arising from a particular social problem.

- **Charity** values a personal or direct connection between donor and recipient – think year-end solicitations for small donations that we receive and respond to from the heart. There are far more charitable than philanthropic organizations, and about half of them in the US do not even meet the annual budget requirements to qualify for exemption from federal income tax. Charitable organizations are typically small, faith- or community-based, actively involve volunteers, and do not depend on big government to further their goals.

- **Philanthropy**, on the other hand, is institutional, big-picture, strategic, and long-term-oriented. It is the investment of private capital for the public good. Strategic philanthropy is focused on solving root causes of systemic societal problems, involves vision and planning, and aims to effect systems-wide change through leveraging investment for maximum impact. Philanthropy does not necessarily imply a personal or direct connection to those in need. It uplifts human welfare through ongoing efforts, long-term programs, and investments that have an influence on public policy.

In a way, philanthropy, when it is strategic, can be viewed as a form of life insurance. It makes long-term investments for peaceful, sustainable, flourishing societies. Such "insurance" minimizes system failures and therefore the need for charitable giving to address crises.

Business, Philanthropy, and Money

The inconvenient truth is that our earth-shattering collective human enterprise has been stewarding the world as if conscious human evolution can be sidestepped. The very fabric of the whole of life as we know it is being pushed to the brink of collapse as safe planetary boundaries are exceeded and our social foundations continue to erode, with ever-greater gaps between rich and poor. Such is the outcome of a financial system predominantly driven by love of money rather than by care for all life.

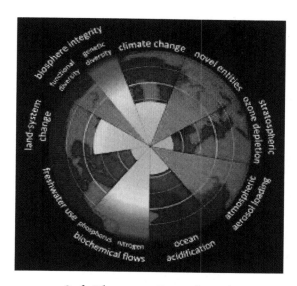

Safe Planetary Boundaries[3]

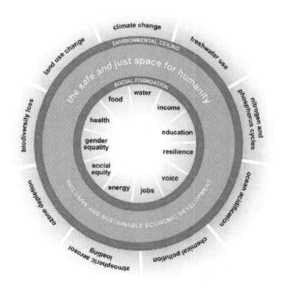

Social Foundations Donut[4]

But there is hope. When we consider that we designed this very financial system, we can see that there is untapped potential to redesign, repurpose, and reinvent it. Important is to understand that philanthropy today is entangled with and restricted by a monetary and financial system that is not designed to operate for the love of humankind and is frequently driven by the need to serve narrow, measurable impacts, *quid pro quos*, and special interests. Hence the increased healthy and warranted soul-searching in philanthropic circles that asks and seeks answers to "What now?"

Billionaire hedge-fund manager and philanthropist Paul Tudor Jones II wants America to avoid revolution, higher taxes, and war by rethinking capitalism and by addressing income inequality. Just Capital Foundation, founded by Jones, encourages businesses to move away from the laser focus on profits that is "threatening the very underpinnings of society."[5] An initiative called Just 100 is designed to benchmark "just" companies in order to save capitalism from itself. Just Capital released these rankings November 30th, 2016. Imagine if a mere 1 percent of capital invested by the targeted 10 percent of the American public that owns stocks were to flow towards companies that reflect what Americans across the political spectrum consider just. Then some $600 billion a year (almost twice as much as all philanthropic giving in the US) could indeed be used to put essential humanity back into capitalism by improving income equality, the environment, and our social culture. Just 100 will appeal to investors as an added tool to demonstrate their commitment to socially responsible investing (SRI), corporate social responsibility (CSR), and environmental and social governance (ESG).

Pocketbook votes by consumers who purchase goods and services from Just-100 companies would add further impetus to making capital flows more charitable and just. Just-100 companies will be better companies to work for, and their employees will likely be more generous in their giving as part of a transformed culture. The initiative rethinks capitalism, making markets work by asking investors to favor being just over maximizing profits – unless, of course, being just also happens to be more profitable. That may well be so (at least in the long run), and has mostly become true for SRI.

Successful activist and fundraiser Dan Pallotta has been on a mission to fundamentally change the way the public thinks about charity, and wants to move the 40-year stagnant 2 percent charitable giving needle by a notch. He explains in his book *Charity Case*:

> The nonprofit sector is critical to our dream of changing the world. There is no greater injustice than the double standard that exists between the for-profit and nonprofit sectors. One gets to feast on marketing, risk-taking, capital, and financial incentive and the other is sentenced to begging.[6]

It is indeed an odd truth that if charitable organizations want to do good they are not supposed to make a profit, and thus remain perpetually dependent on the charity of others. They tend to accomplish not making a profit by keeping overheads low through a combination of modest compensation; limited advertising, marketing, and fundraising budgets; and deployment of volunteers. They try to remain risk-averse while under pressure to show impact immediately and without being able to share profits to attract capital.

Little surprise, then, that between 1975 and 2008 only 201 nonprofit organizations in the US became fifty-million-dollar organizations[7] while anywhere from 125 to 250 companies per year that are founded in the United States (out of roughly 552,000 new employer firms that open each year) reach $100 million in revenues in a reasonable timeframe.[8] With these handicapped rules of the game, the nonprofit sector does not have suitable incentive, nor is it enabled to think big and produce the next philanthropic Google, Apple, Twitter, or Facebook delivering societal change for the love of humankind – that is unless philanthropy is reimagined and its causes can compete with the resources that the for-profit sector can access and mobilize.

Philanthropy (giving) and profit (taking) are flip sides of the same coin. More philanthropy implies more profits, and fewer profits mean less philanthropy – that is if money is the currency of our yardstick and the face value of the pie cannot grow through expansion of true love for humanity.

Indigenous Philanthropy and Wisdom

One of the most, if not the most ancient, beautiful, and singularly philanthropic stream of consciousnesses has been with us since the dawn of time. It embodies a philanthropic cosmology of love and care for humankind. It is the sacred instructions given to certain Native Americans by their Great Spirit at the time of their creation. If ever there was a coherent, philanthropic set of wise rules or self-governing commandments to live by – to keep our compasses pointed to True North across time and space – it must be the following ten, as interpreted by Pachakamak:

Treat the Earth and all that dwell thereon with respect.
Remain close to the Great Spirit.
Show great respect for your fellow beings.
Work together for the benefit of all humankind.
Give assistance and kindness wherever needed.
Do what you know to be right.
Look after the well-being of mind and body.
Dedicate a share of your efforts to the greater good.
Be truthful and honest at all times.
Take full responsibility for your actions.[9]

Observing the current state of our world and our fraying web of life, we cannot but feel deep in our hearts that these commandments were lost to us in translation, fragmented, corrupted, and even purposely quashed by the encroaching culture. The rules we have lived by since at least the discovery of the New World in many ways separate us from the truth, trust, and love evident in these more venerable rules. When we came out of the Dark Ages, first peoples were considered beings not like ourselves; subhuman; to be raped, pillaged, dominated, and worse.

We have since deviated far indeed from True North, but ultimately all of us originated from the same place. There are 370 million indigenous people (aboriginal, first nations, first peoples, tribal people, forest people, hill tribes) across the globe. Indigenous people represent 5 percent of the world population but comprise a disproportionate 15 percent of the world's poor. They suffer from marginalization, land-rights disputes, self-determination and sovereignty issues, and loss of language and culture.

Indigenous people have been Earth's stewards and guardians *par excellence*. Their tribal territories overlap 80 percent of the planet's remaining biodiversity. They are often the first line of defense against encroaching logging; industrial agriculture; and mineral, oil, and gas business interests. They are also at the forefront of many of the critical sustainable-development challenges that require urgent solutions, such as poverty, climate change, human health, and loss of biodiversity. The fate and future of indigenous people are profoundly entangled with the fate of the rest of humanity as one.

Despite all the generosity and wisdom flowing from the original way of life, it is our philanthropic compass that needs serious calibration. Less than 1 percent of global giving to indigenous communities enables them to steward what our way of life has mostly destroyed and depleted and to care for the very Earth that sustains all our humanity. We are called to be in right relationship with – reciprocating, taking responsibility for, and respecting – indigenous people and to embrace them as our full partners and allies in support of a shared, interdependent vision for a secure, peaceful, sustainable, and prosperous present and future. If we love ourselves enough to demonstrate our humanity, our philanthropic compass needs to generously internalize the True North of a higher power such as the Native Americans' Great Spirit.

Genetic studies that trace humanity's ancestry back to when and where we all came from point out that some 5 percent of our DNA across race, gender, creed, and cultural divides comes from the first people who walked on this Earth. We are thus all indigenous in this sense, and carry our ancestral memory deep inside us. Being more generous to native populations is, therefore, tantamount to being more generous to a neglected part of ourselves. It is this giving that holds the real promise and lure by which we can co-create, manifest, and receive a "whole new world."

Technology and Philanthropy

Technological advances pose profound challenges for the field of philanthropy. It often seems we live at the tip a double-edged sword – technology as a tool for promoting the good or the bad, with many shades of gray in between. Technology enables us to drill deep into the core of the Earth for oil, gas, and minerals; to fertilize and spoil our soils, rivers, and streams; and to log our forests, which clean the air we breathe and contain the biodiversity on which life depends.

Pointing our attention to the skies, we control air and space through flight, and can travel to the Moon and Mars, and even peek beyond. Our technological innovations now penetrate deep into the origins in time and space of the universe. Sensors record almost everything that happens on the Earth and above, with real-time data feeds to keep us "secure." And we are on the verge of creating living buildings, living cities, and increasingly human-like robots merging man and machine.

The speed at which technological innovations occur is mind-boggling, ever-accelerating, and increasingly challenging for us and our lagging systems of governance and social technology to keep up with.

All of this comes with tremendous responsibility. We have to wonder whether we are really in control. Without a doubt we can be grateful for many, but certainly not all, of these advances. They have generated tremendous wealth-creation opportunities for much of humanity, though certainly not for everyone. Much technology evolved rapidly at the expense of the integrity of our economic, social, natural, cultural, and spiritual web of life.

All of humanity will soon be interconnected as one via the internet, mobile phones, social media, and a shared resonance within in our noosphere – the sphere of thought, unveiling who we are and where we wish to go. That is hopeful and helpful. As connected human antennae pre-sensing our future, we now have a more direct, immediate, and democratic say about our future in real time, individually and collectively.

How this will exactly unfold is in direct proportion to our overall level of awareness and consciousness and our access to education and responsible media content about how our world works. Our consciousness must outpace the speed of our money-driven world. Raised consciousness must enable the wisdom and power of the crowd to "flow" giving in directions that tackle the enormous economic, social, environmental, cultural, and spiritual challenges we face at the tip of our sword. This can change everything, and philanthropy's servant-leader role in this fast-changing landscape can be the catalytic key. In the sharp words of Bill Gates:

> I often talk about the need for philanthropy to target our greatest needs and spark long-lasting change. Effective philanthropy is no longer the sole province of big foundations that employ teams of experts. With the technology we have today, and with the innovations that are still to come, anyone with an Internet connection, a few dollars to give, and the time to do a little digging can become a more-informed donor. These days, effective philanthropy is for everyone.[10]

Ryan Scott, in a *Forbes* blog piece titled "The Rocket Fuel for your Philanthropy is Technology," stated:

> Employees are also seeking to create a deep and meaningful connection with their supported charities. They want to track their impact, not just dollars raised. They want to see the ways that they're benefiting their local communities and helping to chip away at the global issues of our times. They want to understand how they're contributing to their company's ambitious social impact goals. And as they're seeing all of this change happen in real time, they want to be able to share their stories and do so through their social media identities.[11]

Religion, Spirituality, Reality

Can we bring the often separated parts of life on Earth together to build a more integrated, unified whole? No discourse on reimagining philanthropy would be complete without taking up the challenge of how our imagining processes are limited by our belief systems – our religions, spirituality, and notions of reality. That is, of course, a tall order. But fortunately one can stand on the shoulders of important work and discoveries that weave an emerging story of who we are and what we must do now to create a whole new world. The following paragraphs summarize these entangled strands in a big-picture way. The sources and links supplied invite you to dive more deeply into the material and its subtleties. They open up space for dialogue about the enormous impact the field of philanthropy can have when this collective knowing is applied strategically to address root causes of pressing societal challenges.

- Ken Wilber writes about transpersonal psychology and his own "integral theory," a four-quadrant grid that synthesizes all human knowledge and experience. His work speaks of an evolving, transcending spirituality that honors the truths of modernity and postmodernity, which include our scientific and cultural revolutions and combines them with the essential insights of the great religions.

  Fusing the cultivation of higher states of consciousness of the East with the enlightenment of the West, a more integral spirituality arises that proposes a radically new role for the world's religions, which have great influence on the worldview of most of the global population. Thirty-two percent, or $115 billion, of US donations fund religious causes. Religions are thus in a unique position to heal, if not transform, some of humanity's greatest developmental challenges, in Wilber's words, "from magic to mythic to rational to pluralistic to integral – and to a global society that honors and includes all the stations of life along the way."[12,13]

- Michael Dowd is a progressive Christian minister, author, and eco-theologian known as an advocate of "big history," religious naturalism, sustainability, and climate activism. His work and presentations focus on "what Reality is telling us, through evidence, about how we must now collectively think and act to have any hope of sparing our grandchildren from hell, and sparing ourselves their condemnation."[14] "Reality's" rules represent 10 commandments or "grace limits" (not unlike the concepts of planetary boundaries and social foundations) for avoiding extinction. One can look at these as modern versions of biblical commandments or the ones discussed earlier that were provided to Native Americans by their Great Spirit. "Reality's" rules read and resonate as follows:

1. Stop thinking of me as anything less than Reality with a personality.

2. Stop thinking of "divine revelation" and "God's word" apart from evidence.

3. Stop thinking of Genesis, or your creation story, apart from Big History.

4. Stop thinking of theology apart from ecology.

5. Stop defining and measuring "progress" in short-term, human-centered ways.

6. Stop allowing the free or subsidized polluting of the commons.

7. Stop using renewable resources faster than they can be replenished.

8. Stop using nonrenewable resources in ways that harm or rob future generations.

9. Stop exploring for coal, oil, and natural gas – keep most of it on the ground.

10. Stop making excuses for the inexcusable gap between rich and poor.[14]

Tapping into the power of collective wisdom from the crowd, Michael Dowd invites feedback to help him refine the language he offers. Imagine for a moment the deep transformation that would result if giving flowed in harmony with these commandments. They appear to resonate with an audience across faith traditions.

- Bruce Lipton is a developmental biologist best known for promoting the idea that genes and DNA can be transformed by a person's beliefs, as explained in his recent book, *The Biology of Belief: Unleashing the Power of Consciousness, Matter, and Miracles.* All the cells in our bodies are affected by our thoughts; they have profound effects on our personal lives and the collective life of our species.[15] Tom Campbell is a physicist, author of the *My Big Toe* trilogy, and expert on consciousness. He lectures internationally, describing the nature of our larger reality and explaining our purposes and our connections to that larger reality. Campbell derives a more fundamental science that directly answers the most pressing problems and paradoxes of modern physics.[16] Both Lipton and Campbell arrive at a coherent worldview even though they are trained in different scientific fields: Of relevance to our philanthropic efforts is the unifying truth that we must trust that life's evolution on Earth, whether seen through the lens of biology or that of physics, is at its core propelled by the intention of love.

- Barbara Marx Hubbard is a futurist, author, and public speaker, and the founder of the Foundation for Conscious Evolution. Her motto is "evolution by choice, not by chance."[17] One of her many contributions is the "Evolutionary Story of Creation" and its "Wheel of Co-creation," which provides a vivid, visual map of time and space depicting an evolutionary impulse spiraling upward from the birth of the universe, Earth, life, animal life, and human life to our present co-creative development stage, where we are poised for the emergence of a universal humanity with infinite potential. At the core of the Wheel of Co-creation we find pioneering souls in communion expressing a planet-wide DNA from which "golden" innovations are born through the work of aligned co-creators who address challenges in all domains of life. They include economics, education, environment, governance, health, infrastructure, justice, media, relations, science, spirituality, and the arts. Of Barbara Marx Hubbard's work, Ilia Delio wrote in her book *Making All Things New: Catholicity, Cosmology, Consciousness,* "Barbara believes that Jesus provides an example for us of what human beings can become." She stated:

> All people are born creative, endowed by our Creator with the inalienable right and responsibility to realize our creativity for the good of ourselves and the world. Like Pope Francis, Barbara Marx Hubbard is a Christic Fractal and is generating new fields of conscious action for a more unified world.[18]

- Ervin László is a philosopher of science, a systems theorist, and an integral theorist. He is an advocate of the theory of quantum consciousness.[19] László has long reminded us that humanity is reaching a bifurcation point that will lead to either breakthrough or breakdown. Systems resist change, but can be transformed. How this unfolds is deeply connected to our level of individual and collective consciousness. It has the potential to tip the scale of human evolution and enable a quantum leap. Philanthropy can play an instrumental role in creating holistic solutions that encourage synergistic projects and lead to holistic change. An inspiring example of this is the Giordano Bruno University, a project offering first-class whole-of-life educational content available to all.[20]

- Don Beck is a teacher, geopolitical advisor, and theorist focusing on applications of large-scale psychology including social psychology, evolutionary psychology, and organizational psychology, and their effect on socio-cultural systems. He is the co-author of the "Spiral Dynamics" theory, an evolutionary human development model.[21] Spiral Dynamics describes a master-code process of values and capacities-driven human emergence. Spiraling up from first-tier, instinctual, archaic societies (beige) to magical, animistic (purple) to egocentric power (red) to traditional conformist (blue) to achievement, modern (orange) to pluralistic post-modern (green) to second-tier holistic systemic (yellow) and holarchical, integral societies (turquoise).

Societies can solve their development challenges more effectively by being mindful that underlying memetic values and capacities differ and clash. At yellow we realize that humanity has reached a pivotal stage in its evolution. We appreciate that all our overwhelming problems are interconnected as one and that they must be tackled in an integrated, systemic way, and all at once. Piecemeal approaches and goals are bound to fail. At yellow, a new breed of collaborative, philanthropic "meshwork" enterprise or ecosystem must be formed to facilitate the emergence of peaceful, sustainable, prosperous societies.

The above insights and their telling convergence are provided by remarkable thought leaders of our times working on the cutting edges of science, social innovation, and consciousness. What's important is that they affirm that True North for philanthropy aligns with the truths of their findings, and that we must trust that the expansiveness of love drives human evolution at its core. That is one of the key messages of *Imagining Philanthropy for Life*.

Chapter 6

Emerging Solutions in Search of True North

Marilyn Levin

Philanthropy's Changing Context

With a range of global challenges threatening the future of society, like collapsing ecosystems, economic inequality, health threats, and water shortages, society needs new ways to finance, invest in, and encourage a sustainable future. Responses require unprecedented investments and development of more robust mechanisms for financing change than are currently in place.

The current dramatic pace and scale of change in society, the expansion of our consciousness, and new information technologies that greatly enhance global communication present an opportunity for large-scale transformation in how we fund solutions to the challenges we face. Given the enhanced connectedness of the world, the increasing awareness and consciousness of global citizens, new information technologies, the internet, the diminished importance of national boundaries, and new capacities for entrepreneurial and networked action, we are in a new era of possibility in confronting what troubles us.

The amount of wealth generated from business is also impacting change through increasing assets available for good causes and for expanding the influence that businesses have on the kinds of missions and projects that receive funding. The past age produced the innovation of the private foundation driven by industrial wealth, including the Carnegie, Ford, and Rockefeller foundations. We can see recent innovations in such institutions as the Gordon and Betty Moore Foundation and the Bill & Melinda Gates Foundation, driven by technological wealth. Both types of foundations are representative of the world's super-wealthy billionaire class, which is predicted to transfer massive amounts of resources into addressing current societal challenges over the next 30 years.

Towards the end of the twentieth century, something new began to develop in financing for social change. Investment vehicles emerged that integrated government, capital markets, and foundation resources. Competencies in micro-financing, social-entrepreneur development, crowdfunding, and impact investing also blossomed during this time.

Another accelerator of change is the greatly enhanced sophistication of the field of large-systems change. This developing field is grounded in *complexity theories* and systems knowledge being applied to the full array of change challenges including environment, health, education, war, civil conflict, community economic development, alternative energy, and climate change. It draws from a broad range of knowledge and disciplines and has produced a powerful array of innovative methodologies, tools, and action strategies.

These and other factors are catalyzing an explosion of emerging solutions being implemented on a global scale, resulting in dramatic positive change. It is impossible to be comprehensive in describing the dramatically expanding field of emerging solutions, but a few are explored below to provide an overview.

Root Causes

There is a growing emphasis on understanding and addressing root causes of societal issues rather than directing philanthropic resources towards alleviating the pain and suffering that results from these root causes. The focus on *root cause analysis*, which first emerged in the 1890s, has contributed to significant transformations in society like the eradication of many diseases and the development of many social services for vulnerable populations. However, it has also resulted in the exacerbation of social ills when the root cause analysis is based in the predominant prejudices of the day, such as when eugenics programs sought to eliminate "defective" people from society. As our consciousness rises, an expanding view of oneness and equanimity will hopefully guide both our analyses and actions so that root-cause philanthropy won't reinforce unhealthy norms.

The Middle East is one of several regions leading the way in philanthropy by focusing on addressing root causes instead of alleviating symptoms and by being willing to be patient and wait longer than other cultures for results. The 2015 BNP Paribas Individual Philanthropy Index refers to President of the National Committee for Responsive

Philanthropy (NCRP) Aaron Dorfman's view that many philanthropists under-invest in the highly leveraged strategies of advocacy, civic engagement, and systems change.[1] However, new studies by the NCRP found a 115 to 1 return on these investments, which is far better than returns for funding direct services.[2]

Social Justice Lens

Though significant progress still needs to be made, a "social justice lens" is gaining some traction in the practice of philanthropy. A 2016 report called "The Future of Philanthropy," written by various contributors, captures numerous key considerations:[3]

> Jessie Spector of Resource Generation reminded us that "While a small but growing number of foundations practice social-justice philanthropy, most philanthropists are simply not in the business of confronting the economic inequality that undergirds their power." He also reminded us that the US (and the wealth that has been created there) was founded on the genocide of Native Americans and the forced enslavement of Africans.

> Steve Phillips of Powerpac outlined the numerous policies of the past that created the "inequality that is plaguing America today." He recommended public policy change as "the most effective way to eliminate inequality," explaining that "from a leverage standpoint, far more money can be moved by changing policies than by making individual grants."

As Leah Hunt-Hendrix of Solidaire explained, the two basic steps to address this paradox are to "acknowledge the role that the accumulation of wealth plays in creating the problems we need to solve" and to "understand that giving is a form of power and control, and that we must find ways to share this power." She went on to say that this "means being led by the social movements of our time, and working in partnership with those who are experiencing the burdens of an inequitable society."

And finally, Darren Walker of The Ford Foundation said, "This is an extremely exciting moment for philanthropy" and that we see it in the inspiring and bold commitments of "an entire [new] generation of philanthropists – visionaries committed to driving social justice by putting grantees and beneficiaries behind the wheel."

Impact Investing

Impact investing directs financial investments into companies, organizations, and funds that intend to generate both a financial return and a benefit to society. Research by the Global Impact Investing Network, a leadership group of nearly 60 large-scale impact investors around the world, indicates that the impact-investing market is substantial, with significant potential for growth with $60 billion impact and $11 trillion total assets under management.[4]

Morgan Simon, co-founder and CEO of Toniic, a global network of "early-stage" social investors who provide seed funding to promising businesses, sees "transformative finance" as a way to address some trends of concern for this emerging field. Simon offered Marjorie Kelly's book, *Owning Our Future: The Emerging Ownership Revolution* as a guide to *transformative finance*, which provides resources to projects that:

- are primarily designed, managed, and owned by those affected by these projects

- build local assets that support long-term, sustainable development on the community's own terms

- are designed to add, rather than extract value from communities

- balance risk and return among investors, entrepreneurs, and communities[5]

Transformative-finance projects are thoughtful about how to engage communities not just as producers or consumers, but as leaders and change agents. They create explicit ownership structures that reflect this appreciation and intention. In their structural makeup are mechanisms for direct accountability to the communities they serve. They also ensure that productive assets remain community-owned and that the use of those assets is determined by the community for continued community development. These enterprises are still often led by dynamic social entrepreneurs, but in these cases they see their roles as community organizers rather than top-down leaders.

Collaboration/Collective Impact

Collaboration is accelerating the impact of philanthropy by leveraging pooled resources, catalyzing whole-system views of problems and solutions, and sharing expertise and experience across very diverse skill sets. More and more foundations and nonprofits favor partnerships with other organizations, businesses, and governments to achieve maximum effectiveness. Philanthropic networks of all kinds are serving as increasingly popular ways to leverage money and experience. For example, The Giving Pledge created by billionaires Gates and Buffet was founded to inspire the wealthy people of the world to give the majority of their net worth to philanthropy either during their lifetimes or upon their deaths.[6] And Peggy Rockefeller Dulany's Global Philanthropists Circle brings together about 50 super-rich families from 20 countries to exchange ideas and experiences, with a view primarily to finding solutions to international poverty and inequality.[7]

An emerging, advanced form of collaboration called *collective impact* has also gained traction in recent years. According to *Philanthropy Network*, an article by John Kania and Mark Kramer called "Collective Impact" published in the Winter 2011 edition of the *Stanford Social Innovation Review* spurred a sector-wide conversation about collective impact – the idea that no organization acting alone can solve large-scale issues. Beyond mere collaboration, collective impact is a rigorous approach that is a lever for deep and lasting social change. Foundation Strategy Group continues to conduct research on this strategy and has created an online knowledge exchange site for sharing tools and stories of collective impact in action.

The Green America Center for Sustainability Solutions is using a form of collective impact they call "Collaborative Innovation" to create breakthrough shifts towards sustainability in supply chains and complex systems.[8] They have produced remarkable results in a variety of sectors including bringing solar to the world, removing GMOs from the food system, bringing capital to smaller communities, and moving the magazine industry to recycled paper. They have done so with fewer resources and in shorter time frames than are the norm in the large-systems change industry.

In "Catalytic Philanthropy," in 2009 in the *Stanford Social Innovation Review*, Mark Kramer wrote:

> Mobilizing and coordinating stakeholders is far messier and slower work than funding a compelling grant request from a single organization. Systemic change, however, ultimately depends on a sustained campaign to increase the capacity and coordination of an entire field. We recommended that funders who want to create large-scale change follow four practices: take responsibility for assembling the elements of a solution; create a movement for change; include solutions from outside the nonprofit sector; and use actionable knowledge to influence behavior and improve performance.[9]

Sharing

In the many forms of philanthropy there is an increasing emphasis on sharing resources, research, wisdom, capital, equipment, best practices, expertise, space, and more. This is exemplified by Grantmakers for Effective Organizations, which is a diverse community of more than 500 grant-makers working to reshape the way philanthropy operates. They are committed to advancing smarter grant-making practices that enable nonprofits to grow stronger and more effective at achieving better results by providing grant-makers with the resources and connections to build knowledge and improve practice.

Mechanisms for sharing and gifting in society have exploded, with websites and apps for sharing and gifting just about everything. Philanthropy is catching up to this trend with groups like Fund for Shared Insight, a funding collaborative that believes philanthropy can have a greater social and environmental impact if foundations and nonprofits listen to the people they seek to help, act on what they hear, and openly share what they learn. In the world of corporate philanthropy there is a new call for corporations to share appropriate forms of data with the public sector and social-good organizations as a new form of corporate giving.

Giving circles (people coming together to pool charitable funds) have emerged as a growing form of sharing our philanthropic endeavors with each other to increase the impact of our philanthropy and enhance the experience of giving. According to the Giving Circles Network, giving circles are "a form of shared giving and social investment networking" and "represent a growing trend in philanthropy as community organizations established by individuals are seeking to have greater involvement in their giving."[10]

Venture Philanthropy

Venture philanthropy applies concepts and strategies from venture capital, finance, and business management to achieving philanthropic goals. Various forms that are gaining momentum include philanthrocapitalism, philanthropreneurship, and peacepreneurship.

Venture philanthropy's expansion is due in part to the surge in entrepreneurial wealth and expertise as well as the growing recognition that governments and traditional nonprofits are not suited to the innovative and risky solutions that must be scaled up for society to thrive.

Philanthrocapitalism is the philosophy and practice of applying the objectives and criteria of capitalism to philanthropic enterprises and endeavors. A wonderful example of this at work is actor Paul Newman's business, Newman's Own, which sells numerous health food products and gives all of its after-tax profits to charity. It has now reached about $300 million in donations.

Philanthropreneurship involves applying entrepreneurial approaches and expertise to philanthropy and the development of societal solutions. A powerful example of this is Stars Foundation, founded in 2001 to transform the lives of disadvantaged children and their communities globally. They support strong, locally led civil society organizations that respond to the needs of underserved children by providing unrestricted funding and capacity-building support. They also help such organizations amplify their messages to broaden their visibility and access other sector leaders and funders. Stars' goal is to support the lives of 20 million children and their communities by 2020.

Peacepreneurship is focused on using entrepreneurial approaches and tactics to create peace in communities. According to the Peace Through Commerce website, it "provides a model for achieving sustainable peace called the Matrix of Peace." It teaches how peace is achieved and maintained by an interdependent system of commerce, culture, and laws within a larger consciousness ecosystem.

Especially if the leaders in the venture philanthropy movement are able to ask the tough questions of themselves and address these with courage, the movement is likely to continue to grow and contribute new-paradigm solutions globally. When there is enough recognition that the very model that created the economic growth of billionaires also exacerbated social inequalities, environmental damage, and structural barriers for many, a whole new realm of solutions is possible.

Technology Solutions

As we become more and more technologically savvy, we create platforms for raising funds for and directing funds to causes, issues, businesses, and entrepreneurial opportunities that interest us. New game-changing technological solutions that are transforming how we share and care include online giving and crowdfunding sites, search sites for nonprofits, mobile devices and apps, data analysis sites, and peer-to-peer fundraising through social networking sites. Marketing sites provide discounts for products and services while directing a portion of the cost to charitable organizations. And the expanding list of sites that facilitate sharing, bartering, and trading now enable people to offer each other much of what is needed without exchanging money at all.

The possibilities for technology to continue to enhance philanthropy are incredible. K. Dinesh, Indian philanthropist and co-founder of Infosys, sees technology as "playing a big role in ensuring scalability that doesn't compromise quality while also resulting in better governance and effectiveness and encouraging continual rethinking of current approaches to philanthropy."[11]

Creating the World We Want

As someone who has come to the conversation of philanthropy as both a change agent seeking funding and a regular donor to many causes, it is has been eye-opening for me to witness the transformation of both the practice and identity of philanthropy. Over the last decade the explosion of vehicles that enable people to contribute money (and time and talent) has encouraged people of all levels of vision and resources to claim the practices and identity of "philanthropist."

As we expand our practice of collaborating, sharing, investing for philanthropic impact, and supporting entrepreneurs and technologies that enhance our world, I believe we will experience an enhanced sense of effectively addressing our most pressing societal concerns, and that we have enough of everything we need to do so. I believe this will hasten our process of being more brutally honest in the most loving way with ourselves so that we can own up to the fact that our current levels of giving are dramatically lower than are needed to produce the world we want. Then if we can be present to the plethora of magnificent emerging solutions, we can go "all in" and put our money (and other resources) where our mouths are and actually create the world we are hoping for.

PART III

STORIES OF TRANSFORMATION OF SELF AND SOCIETY

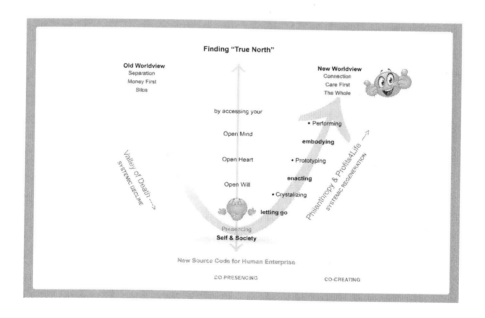

Chapter 7

A Trojan Horse of Love –
KINS Innovation

Susan Davis Moora

My life's work has been to joyously seek out the "Trojan Horses of Love" and bring them together to co-create their boldest missions in service of humanity… and then support them in manifesting these missions. A Trojan Horse of Love is someone who takes on near-impossible tasks, such as having love be the intention behind money, and then manifests dramatic, measurable progress.

This chapter tells the story of one such group of caring, creative, and dedicated people. They were all members of a unique one-year program at Green America called KINS for Philanthropists. The purpose of the program was to help leaders use the KINS method to manifest their destiny paths – their personal missions in life.

At the very first weekend meeting they decided they needed a "meta-mission" in addition to their own individual missions. They fairly quickly identified that they all felt passionate about transforming philanthropy. This shared mission invigorated their bonding from day one, and you are reading the result! Further, the book-collaboration process inspired the development of a potential breakthrough initiative based on imagining Philanthropy for Life.

What makes all the difference in a network's success is a highly conscious energy field, and that was born at the initial KINS for Philanthropists meeting. We chose members who had already found their joy in giving rather than in competing, so they could synergize with each other rather than compete. There are no people as delicious as kindred spirits who share the same life mission and want to collaborate on it for mutual benefit. Hence came the name KINS for our innovation method and networks.

For example, virtually every member of the group needed funding for their own KINS initiative. Rather than ask each other for funding, they sensed that if they explored funding together they would enhance the funding opportunities for all members. And that is just what is happening as you read this.

More than 40 KINS Innovation Networks have been developed over the last 40 years. The networks cover a wide array of fields including solar energy, economic empowerment of women, social investing, corporate social responsibility, local living economies, micro-finance in Nigeria, consciousness, and more. Each new KINS network has enhanced the KINS model from previous networks, so the method continues to evolve and improve.

In 2012 I used funds from the sale of my house to gift the KINS method from my for-profit, Capital Missions Company, to the nonprofit organization I respect the most, Green America. This continues the legacy of linking people on their destiny paths to one another for the enhanced success of all concerned.

Green America's mission is "conscious consumers," as only people using their purchasing power will shift corporate bad behavior. Green America had already been using the KINS method for major initiatives like "no GMOs." They then raised significant funding to create a KINS home called the Center for Sustainability Solutions (www.centerforsustainabilitysolutions.org).

To give you inspiration, I share below the missions of the other KINS for Philanthropists members and myself. Every KINS mission meets the criteria of being inspiring, daunting, short, and measurable!

1. "We are creating a world governed by putting Care First." – Louis Bohtlingk

2. "We are restoring a global economy of reciprocity, inspired by nature and the sacred." – Jyoti

3. "We are sharing indigenous wisdom globally while increasing funding for indigenous causes tenfold." – Barbara Savage

4. "We are redirecting human creativity and financial capital to optimize the conditions for growing sustainable communities." – Stuart Valentine

5. "We are manifesting thriving and measurable microbial solutions industries globally." – Forrist Lytehaause

6. "We are accelerating a peaceful, sustainable, and prosperous way of life by 2025." – Steven Lovink

7. "Our open source, social synergy operating system, birthed in love, manifests by 2020." – Bret Warshawsky

8. "We are manifesting 'conscious sustainability' globally through KINS Innovation Networks." – Susan Davis Moora

We are one of the many groups Margaret Mead described when she said, "Never doubt that a small group of thoughtful, committed citizens can change the world; indeed, it's the only thing that ever has." …And we do intend to change the world.

If you have shifted from your career path to your destiny path of love, joy, and creativity, this book is a gift to you just as the KINS method was a gift to me. For more on KINS and my personal story, please see appendix A and go to www.KINSinnovation.org.

You can also read a recent article that details the workings of one of our most successful networks, The SolarCircle, dedicated to "making solar happen for the world." This article by David Ferris in the September 6, 2016, issue of *Energywire* explores the formation and workings of the group over the last 20 years. It can be found at www. eenews.net/stories/1060042311.

Chapter 8

The Alchemy of
Transformational Investing

Stuart Valentine

M y journey, like those of so many before and alongside me, has
been a sequential, ongoing awakening to the core truth of *non-
duality* and the unfolding wholeness of love. The study of non-duality
– the philosophical, spiritual, and scientific understanding of the non-
separation and oneness of human consciousness – has opened my eyes
to the interconnected nature of our universe. From my childhood roots
in the eco-progressive culture of Portland, Oregon, in the 1970s, I have
watched the evolution of what was then referred to as the *counterculture
movement* expand increasingly into the mainstream through the lens
of the socially responsible investment (SRI) marketplace.

What began in the SRI movement as individuals making connections
between their investments and the often distressing state of the world

is now understood to hold equal promise in transforming investing into a powerful force for good. Our global family is awakening to the understanding that for the human species to survive the twenty-first century, we must redesign the investment process to go beyond the singular fixation on financial profit and become equally passionate about investing for human well-being and environmental sustainability.

The Evolution of the Green Economy Marketplace

Over the last 27 years I have experienced the juxtaposition of my deepening experience of consciousness through the regular group practice of the Transcendental Meditation Sidhis program and my work with investors and speculators cultured in the school of profit maximization. My path of development led me to pursue an MBA from Maharishi University of Management in 1984, which framed up the investment process as an intimate exercise in self-referral, through regular meditation, while teaching the tools one needs to play in the field of business.

Fast-forward to 2016, and it is astounding to see how much our cultural mindset has evolved. Every company in the S&P 500 index is now producing regular environmental, social, and governance (ESG) status reports. A whole new industry of screening companies for relative ESG performance has sprung up. The SRI label has given way to the term *impact investing*, which has served to broaden the field of participants. Now with Wall Street getting into the action, it is estimated that as of the end of 2015, over $6.5 trillion in the US was being managed under SRI/ESG and impact-investment criteria.[1]

The Love Economy

In the context of this shift towards a more whole-system approach to the investment process, it is only natural that we find ourselves in a dialogue about reimagining philanthropy. There is a core, deeply spiritual function that is served within us through the act of giving. This primary human impulse somehow got separated out as a non-economic activity through the adoption of the modern portfolio theory (MPT) investment doctrine. Developed in the early 1950s, MPT measures only the financial component of transactions we engage in through the gross domestic product (GDP) calculation.

However, as my dear friend, mentor, futurist, and founder of Ethical Markets Media, Hazel Henderson, has long pointed out in her diagram of what she calls The Love Economy, GDP completely misses the half of all human activity that is in the form of unpaid sharing between humans and the "ecosystem services" that nature provides for free.[2] (Ecosystem services include provisioning, such as the production of food and water; regulating, such as the control of climate and disease; supporting, such as nutrient cycles and crop pollination; and cultural, such as spiritual and recreational benefits.) Under the mirage of MPT, philanthropy has increasingly been institutionalized and motivated to a large degree by tax-driven incentives, further removing the gifting process from an inspired, direct, relational connection. Indeed, the "business of philanthropy" is modeled as a sector of the economy and measured as simply another component of GDP.

While there is no question that the flow of money through the institutions of philanthropy produces powerful good works for people and the planet, it is also evident that the business model of philanthropy falls short in fulfilling the profound need for heartfelt human connection with others and the natural systems on which we depend.

Find Your Dharmic Destiny Path

Each of us is endowed with the potential for full self-realization rooted in the priceless gift of the field of universal intelligence that permeates the entirety of existence, governs the unfolding of all life, and is accessible through our conscious awareness. Who among us would end this life for a pile of cash? The answer seems obvious, and yet we have created an economic system driven by the "science" of economics that values cash over life.

Many of us are sacrificing what I describe as our highest "dharmic destiny paths" because the demands of capital seemingly supersede the call to realize our core gifts and missions in life. I define one's dharmic destiny path as the path that reflects one's transcendent sense of what one's core purpose is for this lifetime.

Each of us has our innate wisdom and unique strength to contribute to the greater good. Indeed, the whole of creation is in service to a life fully expressed. I define a thriving economy as one in which each citizen is aligned with their dharmic destiny path, which in turn generates optimum conditions for growing healthy communities. I like the image of water flowing downhill to communicate what life feels like when living one's dharmic destiny path: spontaneous right action is clear and there is an experience of a tailwind supporting one's flow through life. Even when there is an experience of being dammed up and blocked, there is courage from the awareness that this, too, shall give way to the next channel of action.

Rooted in this understanding, one is able to minimize the draining effect of resisting what is by being grounded in a deeper trust in the universal power of love. So while the dharmic destiny path requires a release into trusting the process of life, it also requires one to meet the challenges of life with focused awareness and perseverance. In this manner we embrace life in a generative, two-way, creative process, allowing our innate gifts to nourish and co-evolve with the field of universal intelligence from which we all emerge.

Transforming the Hungry Caterpillar into the Butterfly

In the course of my development, and in working with many clients across the full spectrum of investment products from get-rich-quick options and futures-trading schemes to the more integral, conscious investment approach we endeavor to provide at Centerpoint Investment Strategies, I have come to see how we have been cultured to subordinate our dharmic destiny paths in favor of external, consumer-oriented markers of success. As a result, humanity collectively is behaving like a tribe of hungry caterpillars.

There are now about 7.5 billion of us, and Earth is giving us plenty of signals that it is time for humanity to transform all its imaginal cells into a beautiful butterfly mirroring our passion and purpose to create a future we truly wish for in our thoughts and actions, or fail as a species. While it is obvious that humans require basic levels of nourishment and shelter to grow and thrive, it is ever so clear to me that the internal experience of wealth is the real measure of success, and has little to do with how much money or stuff we have.

Countless are the investors I have worked with who have more than ample money yet do not feel wealthy. They are cut off from the wealth of life by their own subjective experiences. Indeed, all too often the dominant relationship to money of a person with high net worth is one of great uncertainty and fear of loss. There is an important clue here as to what drives the Imagining Philanthropy for Life inquiry: Fulfillment in life is a balance between investing our attention inward to enhance the quality of our subjective experiences and investing our money in the marketplace using *triple bottom line* criteria – criteria that include environmental costs in addition to financial and social costs. Further, speaking as a former futures trader, I believe that seeking the externalized markers of investment success while disconnected from one's dharmic destiny path is a very bad trade indeed!

Why We All Need to Exercise Our Philanthropic Gifts

We have all adopted survival patterns to cope with this core disconnection between the demands of capital and the heartfelt desire to live more holistically and in alignment with our dharmic destiny paths. For many investors this shows up as a perceived trade-off in which their innate impulse to share their gifts, especially their money, is put off until they achieve greater financial stability. Further, there is often a perception that philanthropy is the domain of huge charitable entities such as the Bill & Melinda Gates Foundation and the Rockefeller Foundation. After all, the story line goes, "What impact can I really make in addressing [insert your favorite global problem] with my limited resources?" It takes coaching and encouragement to restore the understanding that no matter the gift, philanthropy is a vital, intimate component of fulfilling one's dharmic destiny path.

Without this understanding, what often unfolds in the experience of those with ample financial resources is a fixation on the drama of "the market" and the ups and downs of their investment portfolios. Once hooked into the "got to make more money before I have permission to be more giving" mindset, those with financial resources, and investors in particular, tend towards a feeling of greater uncertainty and a growing fear of loss. This in turn produces a type of "poverty consciousness" that arises from the perception of not having enough money to fulfill the myriad externalized "wants" and "shoulds" that our consumer-driven society dictates as normal.

Nature as the True Central Bank of Wealth and Well-Being

Poverty consciousness arises from our economic model, which has expressly designed scarcity into our financial system along with our collective forgetting about the abundance that is naturally embedded in our human consciousness. We fixate on the Fed or the economy to deliver wealth and security, forgetting that it is the infinitely renewable resource of creative intelligence that flows through our human nervous systems that is the true "Central Bank" of wealth creation.

"Curving back on myself I create again and again," is a clue from the *Bhagavad Gita* that alerts us to the wealth-creating potential we all carry within. The dharmic destiny path framework, combined with this inside-out model through which we experience ourselves as sources of wealth creation, is the foundation for implementing a more whole-system approach to philanthropy and investing. As Charles Eisenstein so eloquently put it, this design is indeed "the more beautiful world in our hearts we know is possible".[3]

Communion, Communication, Community: The Path to an Integral Economic Model

I often comment that I have lived at least 100 lifetimes through the investment experiences of my clients over these last 28 years. Combining these insights with my 35 years of regular meditation, I have developed an investment model called the "True Wealth Tree." The idea is to help investors understand how their unique gifts of life grow out of the field of universal consciousness and can inform their investment choices.

The True Wealth Tree also serves as an empowering road map to lead us out of poverty consciousness and into reimagining philanthropy as a necessary component of our investment plans. The intention is to restore a sense of self-referral to the investment process, the implementation of which is guided by our clearly defined dharmic destiny paths. I believe this can profoundly shift the roles that money and investment play in creating a more regenerative, thriving, green economy. You can see the model at www.centerpointinvesting.com

Chapter 9

Reciprocity, Respect, Responsibility, and Relationships

Barbara Savage and Jyoti

Dreaming a New Dream

We are living in times unprecedented on this planet. It is as if we have been in a deep sleep and are just beginning to awaken. There was a young psychologist who took a group of people down the Amazon deep into the interior of the jungle. Let us share his story, catching just the jewel of its meaning, which emphasizes the times we are in now.

He was dismayed at the trash he saw in the river; at the oil streaks in the water. When his boat pulled up on shore and he got out, he saw an old man standing just six feet from him, looking down the river. The young man approached the elder. He began to express to the old one how sorry he was for all the pollution, for the way we were treating the water, the Earth, her people. The old man said, "The dream is as you dream it."

"But," the young man said, "we have made such a mess."

The old man spoke: "The world is as you dream it. Once you dreamed a most amazing and beautiful dream. You dreamed of lines covering the Earth with things rolling down them going from place to place. Then you dreamed of things flying through the air, taking us all over the world. You dreamed a beautiful dream that then turned into a nightmare."

The young man asked, "How can we awaken from this nightmare?"

The old man replied, "You take one seed and pass it back to the generation standing just behind you, and you'll dream a new dream. It can happen just that fast. For the dream is as you dream it. Dream a new dream." (From *The World Is As You Dream It* by John Perkins, Destiny Books, 1994.)

Sacred Economics – The Fountain – Jyoti's Story

That story inspired me over the years as my life led me to know indigenous people all over the world and create relationships with them. I learned that their wisdom grows from their deep relationships with creation. I learned that nature has an intelligence, and that if we listen, it holds the solutions to the nightmare we are awakening from. I learned that through this intelligence ceremonies had been given to these people that taught them a way of life that brought them balance and cultivated collaboration and reciprocity (the practice of exchange for mutual benefit). I learned that all is sacred. I began to remember the beauty of the original dream.

In the past three years, through following the guidance of nature, an initiative called the Fountain for Natural Order for Our Existence has evolved. The "Fountain" initiative is actualizing a new model of "sacred economics" that combines the most enlightened elements of the Western financial system with the natural intelligence of native wisdom traditions to bring practical solutions to the world's current economic and ecological crises.

The initiative is working to restore the world's sacred sites and return them to the stewardship of their natural indigenous guardians to bring the Earth back into balance. We are using the ancient technologies of ceremony and prayer to receive nature's guidance to this end. We are listening to the Earth herself and advocating what she needs to restore herself. We are returning to the roots of ourselves so that health can be restored.

The Fountain's new sacred economic model presents a way to finally sidestep the mass of negativity created by the world's materialistic and fragmented financial systems and create a new, sacred economic pathway that can unify the world's peoples in collectively creating a sustainable, life-supporting planet in reciprocity with nature. The Fountain initiative is an invitation to help bring about a transformed global society that leaves a legacy of clean air, fresh water, fertile soil, and spiritual harmony for Earth's children. It provides an amazing opportunity to co-create an exemplary model that restores life. The call for collaborative relationship on all levels is imperative.

In its mission to renew a sacred economic model, the Fountain uses ceremony and prayer in accordance with "original principles" of the world's indigenous people. These original principles are based on collaboration and reciprocity and are cultivated through relations and respect. When we make relations with all of creation, everything else flows out from that and a more inclusive foundation is sustained. We understand that all life is sacred and that sacredness is the root of our understanding. Abiding by nature results in a way of life that responds to life, focused through prayer. Each step of this process of moving towards a sacred economic model brings us closer to evolving a new paradigm of reciprocity and collaboration, which are truly the fundamental elements needed in any philanthropic landscape.

During the Fountain's first year, I was led to individuals, both native and non-native, with whom I shared the Fountain vision as directly received from nature. The visionaries gathered together to hold the vision collectively. Each brought to the table inspiration guided by the wisdom of nature. Ceremonies were held and a strong prayer was formulated that would continue to guide this process.

Each visionary had to be willing to accept the evolving vision without expectation of any specific outcome. Each was to understand that the vision would guide us as we peeled away old wounds, outmoded ideas, and the paradigm that has so long encased us in a patriarchal system. Each visionary had to be willing to cultivate their relationship with the Divine so that each seat represented could align itself to original principles. Then, and only then, would we be able to see the "field of reciprocity" that nature intended, so that balance could be restored.

We began to understand that the economy of a system touches all levels of itself – the spiritual, the emotional, and the physical. A "whole" shared system is not just about money, but also about the valued currency. Calling on our rich resource of first-nations' wisdom combined with the knowledge of Western economists, our hearts, and our vision, we came to understand that unity is a medicine for our times – a medicine that is helping us remember. To better understand and see the practical steps that have unfolded, please visit the Fountain's website at www.thefountaincss.org.

Earth is calling us to action, directing initiatives to awaken awareness in the collective about sacred sites, the urgency of clean water and air, and how healthy soil can reverse climate change. It has shown us that the way into the future is through collaboration and alliance building. And as we follow nature, she shows us how all life flows.

A Sharing Economy – Tribal Trust: What Barbara Discovered

As founder of the Tribal Trust Foundation (TTF), I have had the opportunity over the past 20 years to work with many indigenous people who taught me how to be an effective philanthropist. I was initially inspired to reimagine philanthropy as I knew it in order to help the Tharu of Nepal. These were the first indigenous people I ever met.

It was during a critical time in my life when I was at a crossroads. Recently divorced, I had closed my business at a financial loss and did not have any secure income. I was traveling in Katmandu to source stones for a new business. The business was a social enterprise, but it would take years before I would be able to grow the business enough to give back. I embraced the cause of the indigenous people and their ancient culture, who opened my mind and heart to reimagine myself as a philanthropist who would not rely on a Western model.

I took an elephant ride with a Tharu man who opened my heart and eyes to the opportunity for indigenous culture to instruct the world in how to live in harmony with nature and each other. My guide and I had so much to share that we talked nonstop during our three-hour trek through Chitwan National Park. While we chased wild rhinoceros, stopped to observe many rare birds, and listened to the melodic songs of the Tharu women gathering food, I learned about the value of his ancient culture. For example, when crossing the river he pointed out some of his family members harvesting snails. I was reminded that the Red Cross had discovered it was the Tharu custom of eating snails that saved them from dying from a malaria epidemic in 1955 that killed everyone else in the region.

As we continued to compare our lives, I was surprised to learn that my young guide had never ridden in the basket on the elephant in his charge. With my encouragement, we switched places, and I found myself straddling the neck of the elephant with my feet on the elephant's ears in an awkward attempt to direct the huge animal. My guide and I laughed when the elephant lifted his trunk full of dirt and blew it over his head at me in blatant disrespect.

On the ride back to camp, relaxing once again in the comfort of the basket, I learned more about the culture of his once nomadic tribe and the prejudices that threaten their survival, including the sex-slave trafficking of unmarried Tharu girls. Upon my return to the camp I invited the staff to join me for dinner. I wanted to initiate a plan through which I could help the indigenous people of Chitwan. I expressed my desire to give them hope and to help them preserve their rich culture. A grassroots sustainable project for a women's craft collective was soon to be identified, and the Tribal Trust Foundation (TTF) was soon to be born with the mission to help preserve the living arts of indigenous people. My life devoted to *indigenous philanthropy* began.

Since then the mission statement of the foundation has evolved as the organization has grown, learned from the indigenous people it serves, and reimagined the role of philanthropy. The TTF's new mission statement is "to share indigenous wisdom in support of nature and global healing." Our strategy to educate and inspire collective action is based on the indigenous-philanthropy values of reciprocity, respect, responsibility, and relationships – the four Rs – as identified and adopted by International Funders for Indigenous Peoples (IFIP), an organization with a membership of over fifty foundations.

Mohawk Elder Roberta Jamieson shared these fundamental values at the IFIP World Summit on Indigenous Philanthropy in 2015:

> Our indigenous reciprocity is not a philosophical principle, but rather is the way we are instructed to live our lives. This leads us to other principles: the idea that we are guests on this land, not owners; that our relationship to natural resources must be sustainable; that we are part of some kind of cosmic hospitality system to which we can offer little and yet use a lot.

I embraced the concept of philanthropy as a way of life after I understood that philanthropy is not all about money and giving. Everyone can be a philanthropist! As Nancy Brown, one of our KINS for Philanthropists members, articulated so clearly: "Philanthropy is really about healing, with love, in whatever form that energy is given and received and needed."

My first opportunity to experience and subsequently understand the value of reciprocity in philanthropy came within a couple of years of founding the TTF. I was called to a remote area of Western Namibia in the Kalahari Desert to help the San record their ancient way of life on film as a form of protection. Their culture and lives were at stake.

One night I was invited to sit in their sacred circle around a fire. After hours of chanting and trance dancing, the medicine men walked around the circle in an altered state and placed their hands on the bodies of those who needed healing. When an elder healer came to me, he placed his hands on my heart, sending warm, pulsating energy throughout my body. In that moment of receiving, I understood the truth of the medicine man's prior messages to me: "We are one heart beating" and "You carry us in your bones."

We Are Indigenous

We are indigenous. We carry the memory in our DNA (our bones) of once living in a sharing economy in which everyone was valued and respected. We just need to remember our original way of being in the world.

As a philanthropist, I have always worked directly with indigenous communities to gain firsthand understanding and knowledge concerning their requests. The challenge has been to be a messenger between worlds, effectively communicating the importance of diversity and of preserving their ancient cultural traditions, which are frequently in conflict with the dominant culture. The challenge is minimized when there is respect. This is the case in Bhutan, where the government facilitated TTF's work to address the threat to its indigenous people.

The Monpa, the original people of the Black Forest in Central Bhutan, have lived sustainably in the Himalayas for thousands of years. They are traditionally hunter-gatherers, but increasingly, with the encouragement of the government, are practicing both permanent and shifting forms of agriculture. While the government promotes Buddhism and discourages the killing of animals, the Monpa are supported in their efforts to preserve their knowledge, language, weaving, and crafts.

One of the most transformational experiences of my life as a philanthropist was when I traveled to the Congo Basin of the Democratic Republic of the Congo to meet with the endangered pygmies living in the Ituri Forest. I thought the mission was specifically to organize an art exhibition that would bring honor and awareness of the culture; I did not appreciate the urgency and scope of the eco-cultural preservation project until I traveled there. I witnessed the second-largest rainforest in the world being chopped down, and heard the First People's cry: "We are Mbuti. We are children of the forest. We cannot live without the forest." As citizens of the world, we have a responsibility to listen to indigenous people on issues that are closest to them but affect everyone. The exhibition that was organized at the Mbuti's request carries their message. It is a prayer to the world and the ancestors.

The TTF vision "to empower all to remember our indigenous roots and connection to the earth" is also my personal vision as a philanthropist. This vision is significant because it reimagines philanthropy. The vision requires an understanding of the nature of relationships among ancestral cultures, ancestral lands, and spirituality. Inspired by the wisdom and guidance offered by the IFIP's four Rs of indigenous philanthropy and my experience working with indigenous people, it is now my understanding that when we identify ourselves as indigenous to Mother Earth, we acknowledge the responsibility of all humans to participate in caretaking. Remember that a sharing economy was our original way of survival because it promoted living in harmony with nature and each other. As the Western world becomes more conscious of our interconnectedness through technology, we become more appreciative of what our ancestors and indigenous people understand intuitively: We are one.

Benefits of Altruism

It has been scientifically established that there are physical and psychological benefits of altruism. Researchers have found that in terms of quantifying happiness, spending money on others is significantly more effective than spending money on oneself. I can speak to this from personal experience. I love my life and hold tremendous optimism for the future based on a belief that philanthropy offers a new paradigm of giving that can change the world. Our KINS for Philanthropy network is a perfect metaphor. Within our diversity, which represents pioneering technology and ancient wisdom, is a collective, powerful song of intention that offers an alchemical solution for global healing, peace, and happiness through philanthropic initiatives.

I continue to expand my heart and consciousness through my work as a philanthropist. It is my life's journey. My impact has grown relative to the lessons I have learned from the indigenous people I have worked with and love.

Reflections for Dialogue

When we reflect on defining what philanthropy is, we see it through the lens of a whole system. That whole system reflects original principles that gave society a way of life in relationship with the intelligence of nature. From those original days we took a journey, learning and evolving along the way. What we have come to understand is how important it is for the heart to lead the way and the mind to follow.

We must remember that we are all interconnected as we fulfill the dream in which collaboration and cooperation are the energies that create rather than alienate life. We must restore a way of life that cultivates reciprocity, respect, responsibility, and relationship. As Spirit once taught me, "The seed of it all is relations. If you start there, then everything else will unfold. Don't worry."

Chapter 10

Creating a Care First World

Louis Bohtlingk

Viewing Money in the Context of Care

In 1989 I felt an inner calling to come face to face with money in my personal life, to understand our collective issues with money, and to discover ways to resolve these concerns. In order to do this, I needed to learn to look at our financial and economic issues from my heart, overcome my personal fears about money, and understand the fears in our collective psyche.

The impact money has on our lives is huge. Understanding the way in which our monetary system and world economy work, as well as their shortcomings, is not easy. Resolving our issues with money – and understanding how it can serve us and be used for the well-being of all life – can turn the tide for our whole culture.

In 1993 I had a dream in which I saw money and love become one. This completely revolutionized my view of money. By 1997 I understood that by seeing money in the context of care and asking who is in command of money, humanity can move from illusion to clarity about money.

The question to ask is "Do we apply 'Care First' or 'Money First?'" To clarify, "Care First" means we let care (our hearts) lead the way in all money matters and make sure that money serves the well-being of people and the Earth and is not used at their expense ("Money First").

From this simple perspective, an international movement emerged of people young and old from all sectors of life sharing the intention of creating a world governed by Care First. It was formed using Susan Davis Moora's KINS method, and is called the Care First Innovation Network.

Building a Care First World

In my book *Dare to Care*, written in 2009 in collaboration with Hazel Henderson, and my book *Care First*, which I wrote in 2015, I share the principles from which we build a Care First world and how to apply these to the things we care for. These principles are:

1. Understanding Money First and Care First

To build a Care First world we need to look at how money behaves wherever it is being used. We ask ourselves, "Is it being created, allocated, and used in service of or at the expense of well-being? Is this action, this attitude, a Money First or Care First manifestation? Then we can decide to transform the Money First manifestations into Care First in our individual and collective lives.

2. **Receiving the Earth and all it provides as gifts to share with each other**

Another very important part of building a Care First world is the experience of receiving and sharing all the Earth offers as a gift to us all, with the inherent sense that everyone has an equal right to their part of the gift. This sense takes us into the experience of respect for and gratitude for all that Mother Nature is. This is sharing and stewardship rather than greed and possessiveness.

3. **Collaborating from our hearts' intelligence in deep listening and humility**

In order to build a Care First world it is essential to explore how we collaborate with each other. I see this as a process of applying our hearts' intelligence, remaining humble, and deeply listening to each other in a process of serving the common good. This completely aligns with the principles of co-creation through which we listen to the spiritual world, each other, and our planet, and give them all a voice in seeking direction for our lives and our decision-making processes.

4. **Applying Care First to the things we care for**

We care for the well-being of people, our beautiful Earth, and our exchange system, whether it uses a monetary or complementary currency, or no currency at all. This means that we apply these principles to transforming the structure of our present monetary system; social inequality; the pain of needing to make money doing work we do not love; and the lack of protection and guarantee for the provision of the vital needs of home, food, water, education, and healthcare for all people. We combat climate change, the making of profits at the expense of the health and well-being of our ecosystems, and the huge income and power differences in the world.

All these concerns have profound impacts on the daily working lives of most of the world population, though I realize some of the issues can feel very far from home. But if we do not face them, we will stay trapped in an old Money First mode, which destabilizes our world, creates a lot of unhappiness, and diminishes our sense of well-being. In order to create a Care First world, all these issues in all these areas need to be resolved.

The Renewal Movement Worldwide

The wonderful thing is that in the midst of all this turmoil there is a groundswell of new initiatives that aim to resolve these issues, including the huge movements of ethical banking, ethical markets, impact investment, microcredit, basic income, B-corporations, social enterprises, complementary currency, positive money (reforming our present monetary system), and many more. With their ventures they are together creating a whole new tone and foundation of *money serving well-being*. This is turning our old culture upside down. Our world and economies are becoming places where people matter, people and planet come first, and money is a tool to serve people and planet.

We are starting to take charge of our world to direct and decide for ourselves how our economies work instead of feeling victimized by an outside world controlling our lives. The world we define from our hearts' intelligence is no longer seen as a dream. It is becoming the more grounded and sustainable way to run our economies.

Many people refer now to the *purpose economy*, introduced by Aaron Hurst, author of *The Purpose Economy*, which defines successful businesses as those that serve the community and enhance overall well-being. Money, in this process, is a constructive tool (Care First) and no longer the singular focus often harming other things along the way (Money First).

Care First, just like sustainability, is experienced by many as an umbrella for the renewal movement, which describes innovative approaches to our dealings with money. It asks, "Is this action Care First?" regarding every transaction taken within our exchange systems, be it monetary or complementary. Has care been applied?

Care First is becoming reality, and the old is crumbling. We are returning to the basic human values of sharing, caring, loving, giving, and receiving, and leaving our world of fear, greed, selfishness, possessiveness, and desire for power behind.

Sharing the Care First Vision Worldwide

In our Care First Innovation Network called Creating a World Governed by Care First, we are working with the dissemination of the message of Care First in all aspects of our culture worldwide. It is done with the vision that any individual, in any position, in any organization, who grasps Care First and its application, can assist in transforming our financial/economic world and whole culture from the inside out.

The power of Care First is similar to the power of the word *sustainability* as a directive for human behavior. The understanding of Care First can change any person's behavior and attitude very quickly. As soon as they grasp it they can begin to consider its application. Of course there is more to learn, but because it is so simple and practical, it has the potential to spread itself quickly over the globe. It is a language and living reality that can be understood by anyone, whatever their level of education.

We are looking at the possibility of changing the whole system from the inside without the need for the whole system to collapse before change can occur. What needs to collapse within the system is every place where harm is done for money's sake through our Money First attitude.

Through understanding Care First and Money First we can transform these aspects in any organization, government, or individual life, and create systems and organizations based fully on the practice of Care First and sustainability.

Expanding the Care First Innovation Network

Between April of 2013 and February of 2015 a founding group of 100 members in 12 countries was formed. In 2016 more individuals and organizations joined. It is our aim to expand the network to 12 million members by 2020.

As an organism, the network expands naturally because of its validity and the need for it. The organism is based on relationship, mutual respect, listening, collaboration, and service. New people and organizations join with this attitude. In this atmosphere we face our challenges together.

We are building a Care First world through four projects:

1. Creating *agora* (Greek for town square) setups in which we discuss current and social issues and take practical steps to build the future together.

2. School of Care: a place for self-realization, self-development, and education in the application of Care First in our personal lives and society.

3. Expanding the Care First Innovation Network: individuals and organizations connect with each other, work together, and support one another.

4. The Care Fund: examining together how we create financial and other kinds of support for initiatives that are building a Care First world.

These four projects can assist anyone in reimagining philanthropy, finding the strength and conviction of the heart, and applying these to our financial, economic, social, and cultural lives.

The School of Care can become a financially self-sustaining/ fundable proposition to advance a Care First world by supporting those who are at pivotal points in their lives (at the bottom of the U curve) between letting go of Money First beliefs and replacing them with the ethics of Care First.

Care First as an Environment for Philanthropy

Philanthropy can be an action of the heart. We can apply our hearts' intelligence to how we deal with the money we wish to give and/or invest, and let our actions be guided by Care First principles. We can ask ourselves, "Is the way we are using money truly serving our well-being, the well-being of the members of the project we finance, and the project itself; or are we causing a lack of well-being anywhere in our dealings with the money? If so, how we do transform this into a Care First action?"

In the consciousness of the purpose economy, in which we serve the common good and make our best contribution, we can ask, "Does philanthropy start with being passionate as the donor about the greater cause served by the project that is being financed? How does this shape the relationship between the donor and the initiator of the project who receives the financial support?" The financial transaction will surely be constructive when both feel empowered by it and it enhances their well-being. Do the giving and receiving become a mutually supportive/ equal exchange of energy (reciprocity) in which both donor and recipient serve the same greater goal and use money as a tool to serve?

At Greyston Bakery, a leading social enterprise in New York since 1982, money serves well-being in all of their dealings with money. Profits are used to serve the community, create gardens, and develop childcare and work opportunities. Every financial action they make contains the same energy, intention, and love found in any conscious and caring philanthropic transaction. (Find out more at www.greyston. com.) At Greyston they place care first and use money to serve. In that sense philanthropy happens all the time in the full, loving action of the heart! This can be done by everyone, rich or poor, and in exchanges in which money does not change hands.

Chapter 11

Spiritual Philanthropy Awakens - Noomap

Andrea Harding and Bret Warshawsky

No problem can be solved from the same level of consciousness that created it.
–Albert Einstein

It is no measure of health to be well adjusted to a profoundly sick society.
–Jiddu Krishnamurti

Late in the first decade of this millennium, with the growing popularity of crowdfunding, Bret Warshawsky began to explore the concept of a gift economy geared towards sharing individual and collective resources like skills, time, love, and creativity. Philanthropy based on monetary donations felt stagnant, whereas the value added through sharing our energy and attention could be infinitely creative. What if we could create a crowdfunding website that allowed us to share consciousness – a co-creative model harnessing our most profound gifts?

Andrea Harding, a professional and experienced software and business consultant, was on a parallel path. In July of 2012, frustrated with the status quo, Andrea announced she was leaving three businesses behind to pursue her vision of an online co-creation platform called Earth Star Network. In her exploration of the co-creative, or synergistic business model, Andrea came across a blog Bret had written about spiritual philanthropy. This is where our story begins.

Bret's blog, July 2012:

Those like-spirited souls who resonate with Spiritual Philanthropy will perceive intuitively and naturally that we both give and receive equally. Furthermore, it is clear that we have infinite gifts to share unconditionally with each other and the world. Love. Wisdom. Time. Energy. Passion. Attention. Skills. Knowledge. Expertise. Connections. Perceptions. Resources. Currencies. Art. A Spiritual Philanthropist remembers that the separation between self and other is a subjective perception that fulfills a survival pattern in life but is not the entire story.

A Spiritual Philanthropist comprehends our holographic nature of existence; where each individual reflects the whole of reality and the whole reflects back as individuals. This interplay between wholes and parts of the Universe inspires the realization that each of us carries within us a spark of Universal Consciousness which is forever entangled and connected to every other part of Itself. Therefore, serving others is equal to serving one's self and serving one's self is equal to serving others. It's simply the Golden Rule in action, and Spiritual Philanthropists live passionately through this lens of universal consciousness expressing itself as diversity.

Philanthropy (etymologically) is the love of humanity.

Spiritual Philanthropy is the love of love... an act of unified consciousness.

Spiritual Philanthropy implies investing our whole self into life and aspiring towards Return On Intention and Return On Imagination. It does not exclude financial aspirations. Ultimately it encourages the aforementioned varieties of wealth, abundance and prosperity. Spiritual Philanthropy transcends and includes the current triple-bottom-line (profits, people and planet) mind-set into a more integrated stage of cocreative expression; the heart coherence of a holographic economy where expansion and contraction are simply the eternal pulse of gifting and receiving. A breath of fresh air, Spiritual Philanthropy is syntony; an alignment with unified consciousness and therefore alignment with the people, communities, projects and passions that inspire us.

*Out beyond ideas of wrongdoing and rightdoing, there is
a field. I'll meet you there. When the soul lies down in that
grass, the world is too full to talk about. Ideas, language, even
the phrase "each other" doesn't make any sense.*
–Rumi

I am inviting kindred spirits to enter the field of Return On
Intention & Return On Imagination… to invest their Gifts
into the world. This is Rumi's field where we all meet and play
and co-create. The details and structures manifest effortlessly
when we are invested together in love, in unified consciousness.
Solutions arise naturally, effortlessly, when we trust life. When
our souls lie "in this grass" of unified consciousness, the "world
is too full to talk about," and money, business, control, fear,
hate, "doesn't make any sense."

The participation I am inviting is into love itself; where
financial return on investment evolves into its highest
frequency of expression, Return On Imagination. The
edge of cultural evolution is where Spiritual Philanthropy
transcends and includes all current models of business,
investment, economics and philanthropy. Because this is
an integral, synergistic process, we can preserve the best
parts of our world and rest in that which never changes…
unified consciousness… LOVE!

Let us celebrate the arrival of actually living and breathing the
changes we wish to see in the world. Let us invert the processes

we have come to accept as natural like creating structures from the outside in. Let us invert the reductionist, masculine perspective of the parts dominating the whole. We no longer need to build "things." Let us start from the ground of unified consciousness – where we love, and nourish, and support, and where we attend to and cultivate our unity through that expression. The ground of unified consciousness and love is where every world truly begins.

The Core Fractal of Three Find Each Other

The story of our 2012 continues from that same month, July, when we met through Facebook and the journey began, sentimental to say, of two hearts beating as one. We became fast friends, united through shared passion, vision, and intention. By January of 2013 we were in love and we met in person for the first time. We also met the third piece of our puzzle, our best friend, Chris Larcombe. *Spiritual philanthropy* and *synergistic co-creation* have become our life's work and direct experience together with Chris (and the extensive community of networks we are part of) over the past few years.

Like many people currently inspired to realize new models of philanthropy, our inspiration emerged in response to deep dissatisfactions with the status quo. Our quest was catalyzed through personal mental-health crises. We each had severe reactions to the dominant cultural acceptance of competition and inequality, states of tension so chronic that in our early twenties we all found ourselves completely socially immobilized.

Even though we had grown up in different parts of the world and had different life paths, we reached the same conclusion about our psychological dis-eases: they were not indicators of mental instability or a genetic disease; they were emotional gauges of the misalignment of the consensus of "normal" and our own senses of personal freedom and well-being. Our responses to this toxic environment were as natural and organic as the human body fighting off a virus. The insanity was not ours alone, and we wanted to catalyze a reformation.

Inside Out

At the heart of our mission is the expansion of common perceptions of the relationship between our inner and outer worlds. We have become passionate about creating environments and structures that acknowledge the roles that unified consciousness and love play in the way humanity cooperates and shares resources.

Our currently instituted systems are direct mirrors of a collective state of mind. This collective state often dominates the planet because a majority of people share similar beliefs about nature and reality. These paradigmatic systems include overarching attitudes of competition and mechanistic being, convictions of scarcity, mistrust of others, and beliefs that self-interest and control serve us best in a fast-paced world of uncertainty and unpredictability.

So many of these beliefs and their associated paradigms reflect a deep mistrust of feminine, or right-brained ways of perceiving reality, such as granting validity to feelings, intuition, and subtler levels of human experience. Shifts in philanthropy and economics are directly related to shifting our beliefs and expanding our consciousnesses to a holistic worldview. Spiritual philanthropy and synergistic co-creation are innovations that emerged as we began to conceive of the world around us in a whole new way.

Reinventing Self-Organization

Synergistic co-creation is the active application of and lifestyle of our vision for spiritual philanthropy. Humanity, as a collective, tends to support innovations, inventions, and humanitarian endeavors from conventional lenses. Because our most exercised form of cognition is left-brained, we tend to place our focus on how things get done in our culture, prioritizing the material practicalities over the emotional, and using linear processes to determine whether a project is viable.

Synergistic co-creation invites us into an appreciation of *emergence*, a higher-order complexity arising out of chaos in which novel, coherent structures coalesce through interactions among the diverse entities of a system. Emergence occurs when these interactions disrupt, causing the system to differentiate and ultimately coalesce into something novel. Through this appreciation we are able to easily participate in the creation process from a holistic perspective. We collaborate, collectively integrating our gifts and weaving them into a whole which is greater than the sum of its parts. Every experience is a gift, including tension, shadows, and fears. When all of these gifts are acknowledged for their inherent value and purpose, we are able to co-create more beautiful worlds.

Another dimension of our explorations is imagining how our social structures might reorganize themselves if we approached life and society as spiritual philanthropists. This gave birth to the Synergy Space Network and a socio-technological platform we call Metta Hub. *Metta* is a Buddhist term meaning "meditation focused on the development of unconditional love for all beings." Our working hypothesis is that we can self-organize into open-source communities (synergy spaces) that are based on shared visions, values, and intentions.

Our motivations for contributing to these shared synergy spaces come from a natural resonance with each others' desire for mutually beneficial outcomes. In other words, synergistic co-creation is catalyzed through love, collaboration, and inspiration, in contrast to consumption, control, or a bottom line. Metta Hub provides a framework for a "gift" culture in which our desires to contribute to society are felt as joyful celebrations of sharing our gifts, and we are equally inspired and rewarded by seeing the gifts grow in others. The concept of gifting forward is envisioned as a critical piece in this process, in which each co-creator contributes to the project just for the love of it!

We also want to address the whole-system impact of synergistic co-creation: Our gifts, like our passions, intentions, visions, and values, can only synergize interdependently and in relation to one another. There is not a challenge in the world that is not connected to other parts of the system; in truth, there are no isolated issues that can be fully resolved without considering the whole system. This departs from many current perspectives that localize and compartmentalize our models of organization. An authentic whole-system path honors every participant's value and contribution. Our major shift in perception expands the reality of "value" beyond the limited and suffocating quantification of modern life measured in terms of time, money, and hierarchies of perceived rank. We are living a holistic experience in which each person is valued equally for simply being part of a co-creation.

A Changing Global Paradigm: From Flat to Round to Holonic

In 2013 our focus turned to exploring how we could begin to practically implement our ideas across the planet and locally. We discovered immediately that there were very few examples of projects, communities, technologies, or financial models that spoke to our aspirations. What we did discover was Chris Larcombe, a 27-year-old PhD student who had left academia in order to develop technology to reveal society's collective creative capacity through mapping and synergizing information and perceptions. His innovation was a new form of media and communications called *holonic technologies*. Holonic technologies are a way to organize information into a decentralized/central database using information called *holons*, where each holon is both a whole system and simultaneously part of other systems. Conceptually similar to DNA within a cell, or a holograph, in a holon all information is available at each individuated level.

It was a historical "aha!" moment as we were immediately struck by the resonance of our vision with Chris's passions, skills, and genius, especially that of working more actively with perceptions and finding ways to describe whole-within-the-part relationships through social technologies. By the middle of 2013, the three of us had formed a co-stewardship to realize Noomap – a movement and community designed to take spiritual philanthropy and synergistic co-creation to a planetary scale!

What has been revealed since we set out together as a triad is remarkable, largely because it became very clear on our path that the only way to create Noomap was to prototype our methodologies as part of the self-creative process. We have watched our visions and intentions synergize into a greater whole, and we have used the energy of our collective quest to transcend the linear approaches to innovation. Our shared passion for personal and collective healing and for spirit-motivated social action has provided an unbreakable bond, enabling us to heal the stresses presented by time and money. We have answered the call to use more unconventional and emergent means to thrive. This includes unconditional sharing, and exchanging gifts and resources with communities that share resonant intentions and visions.

Sacred Commerce and Holographic Economies

Co-creators and communities that resonate with our vision have gifted many diverse and equally required resources to Noomap. These gifts have included skills, healing, mentorship, money, food, accommodations – even life-defining experiences like our spontaneous, co-created wedding in Australia at the UPLIFT gathering! We calculate that the equivalent of more than £2 million has been gifted to the project in these ways.

More recently we find ourselves co-creating side by side with many networks that share our vision and values. As of this writing, Synergy Hub 1.0 in Rotterdam is being gifted accommodations, food, wi-fi, and various resources by the food-rescue and unconditional sharing project Yunity, a predominantly European group self-organized by over 100 young people and the Meesteren Foundation in Rotterdam, a nonprofit foundation and community that provides supportive environments in which local groups can co-create through sharing.

Noomap itself has evolved significantly over the past few years into a working prototype that can provide the basis for a new kind of internet and radical possibilities for a new planetary, social form of self-organization and perception. Noomap will reboot the internet as we know it, because it can be used to restructure the data landscape by *holonifying* our experience of information. Once this occurs, we will not only have the opportunity to experience information differently, we will also be empowered to reconceive the way we interact online.

One of the most fundamental shifts this will create is the ability to see our planetary organism as interconnected networks working together for all. Using one of Noomap's most powerful and transformative tools, the "Synergy Engine," we can shift from searching the internet to synergizing with each other. This flips our perspectives by allowing us to perceive the potential synergies around the planet as based on abundance rather than starting a project from a myopic standpoint based on competition and scarcity.

The Noosphere Comes On Line

The result is a living laboratory and a tool for positive, harmonious change – like a perception accelerator for consciousness through which we can synergize the perceptions and information around our planet to help make the invisible visible and wake up the *noosphere*, or collective creative intelligence.

Noomap will reveal real-world and visionary solutions based on what's working now as well as what's exciting to our collective and individual hearts. This will initiate an exponential series of synergistic interactions. Noomap will incorporate gaming as well as the latest internet, decentralized, blockchain technologies. The Noomap movement will be supporting, encouraging, and living a lifestyle of unconditional sharing and synergistic value exchange. We are currently exploring the most benevolent and wise ways to inspire Noomap co-creators to become organic, self-organizing, reciprocal, altruistic communities that exchange flows of resources among each other to support a fountain of gift consciousness and a gift civilization.

Chapter 12

Reimagining Philanthropy as Community, Education, and Citizenship

Daniel Blaeuer

For years I understood philanthropy, as many of us do, as the practice of grant-making at private foundations with large endowments. I understood a philanthropist to be an individual who gives money to large charities, attends fundraising dinners in fancy restaurants, and generally provides initial endowments at foundations. Philanthropists were also the people whose names adorn the building where I teach at the local university.

The major problem with the way I saw philanthropy was that the image left me and most people I knew out of the picture. I thought the only way to be a philanthropist was to give money at charity dinners, serve on nonprofit boards, and endow foundations and universities. This image leaves most of us in a situation in which if we have any interaction at all with philanthropy, it is limited to the countless hours spent applying, administering, and evaluating grant projects. It is the image of the rich helping the needy poor.

I share with the other authors of *Imagining Philanthropy for Life* the feeling that this image of philanthropy needs to be reimagined to capture the love of humanity that the word implies. I also share with these authors the belief that only a new, reimagined philanthropy can foster a renewed *practice* of philanthropy capable of unleashing the very love of humanity that is needed to address our collective human challenges in the twenty-first century.

Fortunately, returning to a classical view of philanthropy can provide all the reimagining philanthropy needs. Aeschylus created the term *philanthropy* in his drama *Prometheus Unbound* from the Greek words *philos* and *anthropos* to suggest a love for humanity. George McCully, in his book *Philanthropy Reconsidered*, stated, "The word 'philanthropic' was originally an adjective, not a noun or a verb; it modified not the gift, nor even the giving, but the personal attitude, character, or disposition of the donor."[1]

Aeschylus coined the term to describe Prometheus and his gifts of fire and optimism to his new human, cave-dwelling creatures. In the drama, Prometheus, having stolen fire from Zeus, gave it to his human creations so they could develop practical and civic arts. Prometheus's love was selfless, yet he would suffer greatly for his philanthropic attitude and for his gift. Aeschylus's use of the word *philanthropy* focuses on an ethos or character of the giver and donor. It is important that this philanthropic ethos was not simply or merely for a select few individuals who gave out of obligation or excess wealth, but was an ethos central to the moral and civic life of every citizen.

McCully argued that the philanthropic ethos flourished and reemerged from its classical roots in early colonial America. Colonial America did not have government bureaucracies or large institutions to provide basic public services or to fulfill the many community needs. As a result, the early colonies created voluntary associations to solve problems that required collective action and to address the community concerns they faced on a regular bases. The ethos of philanthropy was expressed in colonial America by colonists who engaged in private initiatives that often required private expenses of time, treasure, and talents for the collective well-being of the larger community.

KINS and the Giving Ethos

I was first introduced to philanthropy as a community organizer working closely with communities to solve collective problems. Community organizing involves bringing people together to discuss community challenges and share resources to address them. Community organizers often work without institutional or governmental support to facilitate private citizens as they develop and generate the resources needed for a community initiative. In this way community organizers are engaged in philanthropy because it involves private initiatives for public good.

As a community organizer in Tampa, Florida, I was invited to attend a KINS Innovation Network. Having been a dialogue facilitator and organizer for years, I understood Susan Davis Moora's basic ground rules for a KINS network to insure a healthy conversation and productive workgroup. Moora's work in group facilitation and networks focuses on the role of self-work and personal growth in the process of giving and community service. In this way, the KINS method seeks to attract people with high credibility and integrity in their communities and constituent groups while providing opportunities to grow and develop within the networks.

The first weekend retreat in the KINS method – a founders' retreat, involves periods of self-reflection and meditation as the group collectively tries to develop a mission statement and an intention for their time together. I understand Moora's work in KINS to have largely emerged from her early career as a community organizer, and that a large part of the KINS method involves the slow work of generating a community around a shared mission.

In the KINS networks there is a unique understanding of philanthropy: Everyone who operates and interacts with a philanthropic ethos of loving all humanity is a philanthropist. Each person's gifts are valued for what they are and what they bring to the group. *Philanthropy* describes the character of the people who give of themselves to foster ways to solve collective and community concerns. What impressed me the most about the process was how KINS networks asked every participant to bring their highest and most noble selves to the group and to offer their unique gifts of time, treasures, and talents. KINS networks are examples of how philanthropy is reimagined to focus on the expression of community and our highest selves.

Philanthropy and Education

At the initial KINS meeting in Florida I was shocked and delighted to find Ryan, a student of mine from a Community, Culture, and

Communication course I had taught a few years back. The class involved service learning and required a significant community project. My former student did his service-learning project with an organic farm, and I remembered that he must have decided during the semester that farming was more exciting than my lectures. In any case, Ryan found his passion and was now an emerging leader in the organic farming community, starting small organic farm businesses across town. With Ryan sitting in the circle, it got me thinking that it would be exciting if the KINS method could be adapted to a university classroom by bringing diverse students into a group to develop a KINS Innovation Network. It could also ideally connect those students with local funding opportunities.

At the time of the first meeting, I was just finishing my dissertation and beginning a career as a research professor. I did not know then how my experiences in KINS could connect with my career path, and was fearful that it was a distraction. I regretfully left the KINS network.

My chance to reconnect with the idea of community giving emerged three years later when two philanthropists approached the university to invite proposals for how a university department could develop a class in philanthropy. The goal of the philanthropists was to create an "ethos of giving" in our students. They wanted students to understand the work of philanthropy and the responsibility that comes with it, to understand the work of nonprofits, and to consider careers in nonprofit organizations. The Miami philanthropists were inspired by similar philanthropy classes at several major academic institutions, and felt the program would be even more important in the South

Florida community because it was just beginning to develop a robust network of philanthropy and was struggling with developing strong attachments to the city.

Knowing they had two goals in mind that were unique, the philanthropists issued a challenge to university departments for a proposal. Their challenge resulted in the simple idea that the Department of Communication would use the classroom of one of its existing courses as a place where students would work directly with a community nonprofit to design a series of projects to compete for funds at the end of the semester. The philanthropists' gift would simply pass through the university's foundation (as a fiscal agent) on its way to the eventual community nonprofit. In turn, the nonprofit would invoice the university for the cost of administering the grant.

The design is simple and easy to replicate in communities. Each semester a class is chosen for an applied writing and communication course directed to a community challenge. During the semester students identify community needs and opportunities while working with local nonprofits. Students work in teams using their skills as writers, researchers, and advocates to write project proposals for funding at the end of the semester. The instructor invites nonprofit leaders to a final class presentation to choose the winning organization for the funding. Although disheartening to see some projects lose, it is helpful to have the judges suggest avenues by which runners-up can develop projects and point to opportunities for additional funding.

Now, on the first day of the class, I surprise the students by telling them that this semester they will become philanthropists and work with community groups to develop projects and proposals to make South Florida a better place. I tell them I will coach them in the process, provide consultation, and evaluate the class just like any other class with assignments, tests, and learning objectives. The only difference – and it is significant – is that this semester their classroom learning and assignments will all be directed towards giving away a small grant to make South Florida a better place. I insist that my evaluation and the class grade are independent from the actual award of the funding. As an instructor influenced by ideas of community giving from my experience in a KINS network, I follow a humanities and classical approach to philanthropy by focusing the class on debate, discussion, and civic inquiry. The students begin with discussions of their personal connections with giving and volunteering. They then discuss community concerns and issues by making student presentations. The presentations are the basis for students to self-organize into groups to work on community-based projects. They then write project updates and case studies and conduct site visits for their organization and problem area.

The philanthropy class challenges students to understand that civic life requires more than just giving back to a community after they are successful, and that it indeed begins with an ethos to love all of humanity and to allow this ethics of care to guide their work and career choices. In my class, like the KINS method before, philanthropy is rooted in the process of conversation and self-discovery that emerges as people come together to discuss their community and their desires for their community from their highest and most noble selves. Focusing on teaching and learning about the self and community means that education becomes character development. The philanthropy training involves changing and growing into the type of person who, like Prometheus, gives of themselves often at great cost to make our world a better place for all of God's children.

The reimagined philanthropy I suggest here is in stark contrast with the image of philanthropy that emerged at the beginning of the twentieth century, when industrialization was creating massive wealth and facilitating private family foundations. A classical notion of philanthropy rooted in conversation and community service accomplished directly by individuals is a far cry from the current standard image of philanthropy as the wealthy few helping those less fortunate. Learning to do philanthropy means more than just learning to conduct site visits and due diligence. It means learning to become a citizen. Philanthropy is becoming something governed by friendships and mutual interests rather than contracts and obligations. Most important, reimagined philanthropy is philanthropy everyone can practice.

Chapter 13

Reshaping the Field of Philanthropy: Flow Funding in Action

Marilyn Levin

May the rivers of wealth be undammed and flow freely over the earth. May the gifts move through increased hands until all people experience the abundance of life.
–Marion Rockefeller Weber,
Initiator of The Flow Fund Circle

Creative Disruption

A heightened focus on creative disruption to the status quo is currently reshaping many aspects of our culture, including the field of philanthropy. The Indie Philanthropy Initiative (IPI), with a mission of "creative disruption to the status quo of funding" is one of a growing number of groups that are leading the way in this disruption through decentralized, daring funding alternatives. As their website notes, "Some Indie Philanthropy practices have been around for decades while others are emerging in real time." This group is working to bring radical ideas into the mainstream, changing the face of philanthropy, and adding much needed diversity and creativity to the field.

IPI shares nine philanthropic practices on their site and notes these as being some of the most accessible, successful, and collaborative practices:

- Community Based Decision Making – empowers community members to make funding decisions

- Funding Individuals – channels money directly to individuals instead of organizations

- Funding Start-Ups – seeds dreams, emergent ideas, and new projects and organizations

- Giving Circles – where people who share passion for a cause can pool money and expertise

- Micro Granting – seeds new work and seizes windows of opportunity

- Partnerships – collaborates with other organizations on funding

- Spending Down – intentionally grants more than is being replenished

- Indie Investing – directs investment capital to enterprises that fit their mission

- Flow Funding – entrusts individuals or organizations to gift the funds to others

To read more about each of these methods, how they work, what challenges they hold, and what benefits they have, visit their IPI Toolkit at: https://indiephilanthropy.org/toolkit.

Flow Funding

Flow Funding, a great example of creatively disrupting the philanthropic status quo, chooses visionaries, most of whom have never given money away before, to disburse funds in intuitive and heartfelt ways. They focus equally on the process of giving and its effect on each Flow Funder and recipient. Flow Funding is thought of as a healing-arts form of giving.

A wonderful example of Flow Funding in action is shared by the Aepoch Fund on the IPI site (www.indiephilanthropy.org/stories/aepoch-fund). From the Aepoch Fund page:

"As a small foundation with a big mission…it wasn't feasible to be experts in and connected to all the sectors, issues, communities they wished to fund. We knew community leaders and organizations had the trusted relationships and a canopy view to know what's most important to fund in their particular area of expertise. We also valued inclusivity and sharing philanthropic decision-making power with more people. In addition, we felt it was a strategic and effective way to reach emerging work, at just the right moment when a small amount of money could make a big difference.

"Most of our Flow Funders were first grant recipients, whether through an organization, or as individual artists and activists. So we had already established a trusting relationship...Most of these people and projects [that were funded through the flow funds] wouldn't have made it through conventional foundation application hoops – perceived as too small, too risky, or too new. With the Flow Funders vouching for the integrity, potential and importance of the work, we were able to seed possibilities outside of traditional philanthropy's reach."

For example, they funded the Movement Generation Justice & Ecology Project (MG) for two years before offering them a Flow Fund.

"This was such a perfect set-up! MG had some amazing collaborative partners in their network who were taking on innovative and experimental projects designed to support a just environmental and economic transition in Bay Area communities. MG was in a unique position to solicit ideas and evaluate the suitability of these projects for seed funding. We allocated $20,000 per year for two years for MG to distribute to the most creative and effective ideas emerging from its network."

A Healing Art

Flow Funding is a healing-arts form of philanthropy that honors spontaneity and creativity. It is free from the traditional, more linear type of philanthropic guidelines, and is based on trust. It has a transformative and empowering effect on each Flow Funder. Flow Funding's founder initially chose Flow Funder visionaries to give away

$60,000 over a three- or five-year period. Since Flow Funders are not known donors they have the creative freedom to notice the people and projects that really resonate with their hearts. Flow Funders give support spontaneously and intuitively in a meaningful way. They are all healing artists of generosity.

The idea for the Flow Fund Circle came about 25 years ago after Flow Funding's founder, Marion Rockefeller Weber, took a vacation from her philanthropy for a year. It became very clear that she did not want to return to the constricted form of philanthropy she had been practicing. While making out her will it came to her that she would enjoy giving gifts of money to friends, who she had supported previously, to give away. Everybody she asked told her that they would be thrilled to give money away! And so flow funds immediately began to go out all over the world in ways that she could never have imagined.

And from that moment on funding became a creative outlet instead of a duty for her. There were, of course, surprises and challenges along the way but she had a practice of opening a discussion of Angeles Arrien's four learning questions when issues arose:

- What inspired you?
- What challenged you?
- What surprised you?
- What moved or touched you?

Learning by Doing

The surprises with Flow Funding were perhaps the most energizing for those who participated as they allowed creative insights to rise up from the group and helped shift the understanding of what they were doing collectively to a new level.

Marion also learned early on that it has to be the right moment in a person's life to be a Flow Funder. If a person is still struggling to live sustainably, it is too hard to be given money to give away at a time when they are needing to find their own money to live on.

She believes that traditional foundations and philanthropists might find that staff burn-out will diminish and the old patterns of funding will soften, with new potentials rising spontaneously and in a refreshing way, if they introduce Flow Funding in a small ways, perhaps by giving their staff money to give away.

She believes that when the process of giving is shared, it is more relaxed and more fun. As she used this new giving approach, she found that the walls that sometimes had been built around her wealth (by herself and others) began to recede. Money began to flow in a natural and healing way from her to the Flow Funders and out in the world. She believes that "since we all long to feel connected and free from isolation and to feel the flow of our generosity deeply, creating a flow fund circle can catalyze the sense of connection and contribution in any group of people committed to philanthropy and giving."

She also feels that "Flow Funding is an approach that can end the constrictions of duty, alienation, and burn out, and let in the fresh air of discovery, adventure, warmth, mystery and friendship." This form of philanthropy has proven effective because it is based on trust and the wisdom of the circles of participants, and because outreach and discoveries are all transparent and shared.

When reviewing the Flow Funding website you can see that small amounts of money given with care and trust at the right moment can leverage an impact much larger than the dollars. This allows for seeding projects on the leading edge of new approaches before the concepts are more widely embraced. Having some funds to distribute gives Flow Funders leverage to grow the legitimacy of new approaches because sometimes the credibility that comes from receiving a grant is even more significant than the actual dollars.

Money is often associated with power, and can give legitimacy to ideas. This fact can either be abused or used consciously for community empowerment. Much of formal philanthropy seems to focus on "safe" and "proven" approaches to social betterment, or in some cases even seems more intent on funding the status quo. From the Indie Philanthropy Initiative and Flow Funding perspective, philanthropy could be a huge support of the bold and radical actions needed to bring humanity near the thriving and healthy economy and ecology that we know is possible. Practicing Indie Philanthropy and Flow Funding empowers communities to reflect on and build on the creativity, wholeness, and diversity of the community in ways that can be more fun and fulfilling than traditional philanthropy.

For more on Indie Philanthropy – www.indiephilanthropy.org.
For more on Flow Funding – www.flowfunding.org.

Chapter 14

On Philanthropy and Profits4Life

Steven Lovink

The Trojan Horse of Love

We were gathered in a circle on the calming eastern shores of Chesapeake Bay, one of the largest tributaries in the United States and world, its history so beautifully described in John Michener's book by that name. Situated symbolically yet firmly in our midst was a Trojan Horse of Love.

We had come together as invited members of a new KINS Innovation Network. It is a tried and proven method for creating unique, transformative initiatives of self and society that benefit all participants, with generative ripple effects far beyond. The KINS method is designed to create wins for everyone within a safe container of mystery and anticipation of the unknown. The method and its success is beautifully described for everyone to hear its song in a book written by Susan Davis Moora entitled *The Trojan Horse of Love.*[1] The KINS method was gifted in 2013 to Green America as one of its core programmatic, pillar initiatives to accelerate system-wide transformation at scale. You can see the adaptation of the KINS method to serve large-scale systems change at the website for the Green America Center for Sustainability Solutions: http://centerforsustainabilitysolutions.org.

Our ten KINS members came from a wide variety of backgrounds, skill sets, and careers. Quite a few of us knew each other. Some of us had already connected through our respective networks of colleagues and friends, while others were meeting for the first time. What unified the group instantaneously was that all participants had either been working for many years on unique kindred initiatives or had started working on a groundbreaking idea. All shared a philanthropically oriented mission to advance deep transformational change of self and society fueled by the expansive power and connective tissue of love.

Our collective challenge as the KINS for Philanthropists would focus on the theme of reimagining philanthropy. At least some of us, including myself, were somewhat puzzled as to why we had been invited or what we might be able to contribute; we did not necessarily think of ourselves as philanthropists. But that is the secret of the success of KINS networks. Over time it would become apparent that it was this very puzzle of "What is philanthropy?" "Who is a philanthropist?" and "How can we reimagine philanthropy?" that represented the Trojan Horse of Love in our midst and from which the idea for this book was born.

Fast-forward to the present, and I must express that the process has been deeply rewarding, and I believe the greatest gifts are yet to be unpacked and released.

I was struck from the beginning of our calls and meetings by the creative tension between my own puzzlement, presence, and role in the group and what must have been the other members' quite similar sentiments. It seemed we had come together to tease out a win-win "meta mission" – an overarching goal – for accelerating our respective initiatives as parts coming together to form a far greater whole. But I also felt that the individual KINS missions we would read out to each other as they evolved over time somewhat hid our meta mission from plain sight.

The connection between the wisdom and knowing that would be imparted about reimagining philanthropy was really intriguing from the outset. It felt like we were all looking for a game-changing form of consciousness-infused philanthropy, and that sparks would fly!

On Becoming a Philanthropist

I never really thought of myself as a philanthropist, at least not in the sense traditionally attached to the word. The word *philanthropreneur* – someone who brings a creative or entrepreneurial approach to philanthropy – seems more fitting. During the first ten years of my career I started, raised money for, built, and sold an electronics signal processing business. The next decade was devoted to providing finance and venture-development services to mostly early-stage ventures, working with founders and private investors with a focus on information technology, life sciences, online education, ecotourism, and nature conservation.

By the late 1990s I found myself more and more engaged with figuring out how financing can be mobilized in support of triple-bottom-line initiatives that take into consideration people and planet in addition to profit. If you think raising money for start-ups is difficult, financing and developing ventures that wish to do well by doing good was even harder, especially then. It was a time when I traveled extensively to South America, including deep into the rainforests of Colombia, where I spent time with an indigenous community and their shaman. I learned much in the rainforest. I also started to look at the bigger structural and systemic picture of supporting the emerging triple-bottom-line sector, which led, among other things, to the publication of a report called "Financing Biodiversity Conservation" for the Inter-American Development Bank.[2]

In 2003 I published a consultation paper called "Eco-Insurance for a Sustainable Future," a proposed financial mechanism for mobilizing needed resources for proactive investments in life-supporting ecosystems. Investments with such a focus were then and still remain highly undercapitalized. The "eco-insurance" concept incorporated an early form of crowdfunding and a proposed "World Conservation Bank" governed for and on behalf of global citizens as primary beneficiaries. Eco-insurance was an idea ahead of its time in a world needing to grow up and wake up; it became a dormant seed for potential change.

The first signs of my philanthropreneurial nature emerged in 2004 when I co-founded the Institute for Environmental Security in The Hague. In 2015 this institute organized the first Planetary Security Conference in the Peace Palace in collaboration with the Netherlands

Ministry of Foreign Affairs. (At least two more such global conferences will be organized by a coalition of partners including the Institute for Environmental Security.)

Then in 2006 I founded Planet2025 Network as a nonprofit with a mission to advance a peaceful, sustainable way of life by 2025; and in 2009, Power of One. To this day these small organizations remain the main outlets for my philanthropy. It is expressed by contributing my time and creative entrepreneurial ideas to the eventual realization of their important missions, and more recently by my writing featured at www.lovink.life.

You see, I believe a new and better world is poised to emerge from a spirit of community and entrepreneurship in service with the whole of life. When community and entrepreneurship are creatively combined in service with the whole of life, unimaginable potential can be unleashed to tackle humanity's greatest challenges.

On Profits4Life

When breakthrough ideas are born in the hearts and minds of inventors, innovators, communities, entrepreneurs, or a combination thereof, they usually set up a corporation that maximizes profits for its shareholders and investors. If we look at our financial and economic system as a whole, the majority of business is conducted this way, albeit at the expense of our now severely undermined economic, social, natural, cultural, and spiritual fabric of life. Financial markets look primarily at profit potential for private entities as opposed to wealth (well-being and health) creation or public good; capital flows to those corporations that promise to generate the greatest windfalls, right?

When we further consider how money is created out of thin air and an offsetting debt is entered into the books, additional impetus is generated for investing in companies that yield high returns that might deliver limited benefits to society, or worse, damage or destroy the Earth. So how can we put soul and purpose into our corporations beyond money – the only yardstick for performance? How can corporations be established with licenses to not only operate for profit, but also operate to generate more needed social, natural, cultural, and spiritual forms of capital and resources? For this we must change the game.

The best moment in which to intervene is when new businesses are formed, especially if they seek to provide products and services that are designed to serve the whole of life. Such responsible, intrinsically sustainable products and services are bound to enjoy increasing market demand. More whole-system-oriented opportunities for success will emerge as our web of life continues to fray; it is already happening.

Now consider that any entrepreneur has the prerogative to start a new business as a philanthropreneur by sharing the profits from success with the community being served, which in turn supports the new business, financially and otherwise. Will such a business attract funding as it lowers profit potential for investors? This depends on the soundness of the management team and business plan, the ability of the business to address a pressing need (as in any business), and the ability of the business to replace conventional sources of capital with a community of investors and a "crowd" willing to energize the business with gifts and other forms of low-cost financial resources.

An exciting window of opportunity exists to change the game by catalyzing whole-system entrepreneurial enterprises with philanthropic gifts energized by Profits4Life, a voluntary, systemic, and self-governing financial "DNA" that can be embraced throughout all we pursue to realize our fullest evolutionary potential. The aim of Profits4Life is to rebalance economic, social, natural, cultural, and spiritual sources and flows in society, restoring the very fabric of life. It takes a *quintuple-bottom-line* approach. At the heart of this financial DNA – a new source code for human enterprise incorporating an appreciation for the gift of life and employing an ethics of care – is a Profits4Life agreement between shareholders, partners, or members of an organization and sources of philanthropic or low-cost financial resources. The Profits4Life agreement binds the parties as to how profits from the success of an enterprise will be shared and directed to flow.

You can envision Profits4Life as a Promethean gift of fire and hope designed to uplift the human condition. It is a new source code for transforming the way money flows – a business approach that transforms corporations from the inside out through profit sharing. It's a systemically oriented approach to philanthropreneurship with very smart impact and the potential to enable the emergence of a local-to-global, whole-system, entrepreneurial ecosystem. As a philanthropic crowdfunding mechanism, it can catalyze community and entrepreneurship in service with the whole of life. This enables an upward spiral empowering transformation of self and society, energized by philanthropic gifts.

It may well be possible to integrate the Philanthropy for Life and Profits4Life approaches as a source code for human enterprise into blockchain technology and crypto-currency (digital encrypted currency) innovations. This could have the potential of deeply transforming and disrupting the quality and quantity of our philanthropy, profit-making, and investments on foundations of transparency, trust, low transaction costs, and smart Profits4Life contracts. The approach aims to build a thriving entrepreneurial ecosystem operating in service with all of life to deliver shared prosperity and address humanity's most pressing challenges at the necessary speed and scale. "Giving Unchained: Philanthropy and the Blockchain," by Rhodri Davies of the UK-based Charity Aid Foundation, provides an idea of what a blockchained future may hold for charitable organizations.[3]

There is not room here to discuss how the Profits4Life vision works in detail, but a brief overview was provided in a recent *Kosmos Journal for Global Transformation* essay called "On Living Business." A forthcoming book, *On Profits4Life: The Alchemy of Money, Love, and Life,* to be released in 2018, will convey the what, why, and how. Suffice it to say that the Profits4Life approach can most easily be adopted by establishing (or converting to) a business that integrates Profits4Life principles and applies them to the general and specific public benefits defined in its articles of incorporation.

Community, Entrepreneurship, Philanthropy

For a very long time, as so many of us do intuitively, I have felt that by giving generously we receive even more than the value of the gift, both individually and collectively. There are many misconceptions or "misgivings" about giving. "How wonderful it is," I have thought often and with gratitude, "to collaborate with amazing colleagues to test and refine how a whole-system-oriented solution like Profits4Life can not only contribute to reimagining philanthropy but also reinforce a key building block of my own vision – that of catalyzing community and entrepreneurship through gifts and in service with the whole of life."

My research through time and space for stories, explanations, and the origins and shadow sides of philanthropy unwrapped many gifts. It reconfirmed my feelings that as part of the energetic exchange that occurs between giver and receiver, a material and spiritual relationship is formed that includes the power to create transformative impact or a disabling lack thereof. A deep understanding of this relationship is key.

The mythical, archetypical story of Promethean fire and hope is deeply embedded in the collective consciousness of humankind. It is a compelling, inspirational story explaining the meaning and purpose (the ethos) of philanthropy. It also provides a solid foundation for exploring how philanthropy can be reimagined in a profound way. I suggest this not only in regard to Prometheus's long-standing Western, Greek, historic, and philosophical roots (towards which I must confess I have some no-harm-intended cultural bias). This story also reflects like interpretations of the innate love of humanity found in the languages, symbols, and traditions passed on verbally by original and free first nations and people, for example by the old texts of the Upanishads, the Sumerians, the ancient Egyptians, the authors of the Bible (specifically Genesis), and the Mayans. Most leading world traditions tell the story of Prometheus in their own special way.

What is perhaps even more striking about the Promethean story is that centuries later it so aptly mirrors the precarious condition of humanity today. Fire and hope must be symbolically stolen from an all-powerful, angry god – the god of money, banking, and finance – for the love of humankind. Only then can we become truly human. Not unlike in the past, we seem to be dwelling in caves of limited belief systems (our monetary system, for one), afraid and kept in the dark (by war, conflict, poverty, scarcity, insecurity, shame, blame, separation, and environmental decline), and obscured from light (worldviews that integrate the hidden connections of all life, peace, freedom, prosperity, democracy, justice, and happiness). Dwelling in these caves is preventing our conscious evolution. If our past, present, and future are entangled in the now, then now is certainly the time to invoke a modern-day Promethean act of loving kindness. This act can again uplift the human spirit and condition with fire and hope through raised consciousness that opens up limitless possibilities for reaching our fullest human potential.

On Philanthropy for Life

Everything in life starts with a gift. The Big Bang some 3.8 billion years ago was certainly a universal gift out of nowhere, and so has been the ever-expansive symphony of life since, in all of its diversity, including the gift of our very own lives – a free ticket to a very exciting ride! When a gift is given, it is up to the receiver to accept it with deep-felt reciprocity, respect, and responsibility – in other words, *in right relationship.*

It is safe to say that the gift of life that humans received has been poorly handled, even squandered. We are *out of right relationship* through not caring for ourselves, each other, and the whole symphony of life. I believe the existential lesson we are all learning is how to more consciously receive, care for, and be grateful for the gift of life, something first nations and people have always deeply appreciated and honored. We impair the circular flows of universal expansive love when we persistently take more than we give, and when gifts are part and parcel of a conditioned *quid-pro-quo* exchange.

We must understand that gifts are energetically linked to the intention of the giver and the need(s) of the receiver. Givers, not unlike receivers, can be impaired in their ability to be in right relationship with the other. As we saw in chapter 5, giving, in ascending levels of right relationship, is: giving grudgingly, less than one can afford, generously when asked, before being asked, anonymous for the giver (but not the recipient), anonymous for the recipient (but not the giver), anonymous for both, or assisting the recipient in becoming self-sufficient and enabled to give as well.

Helping someone become self-sufficient through, for instance, education and training, teaching specific skills (teaching a man to fish and more), or setting someone up in a business, can indeed be considered the highest form of giving for the love of humankind, especially when giver and receiver deeply respect and align their relationship with the whole of life, nature, and the immutable laws of the universe. When we think of foreign aid especially, our customs of giving, intended or not, have been culturally biased towards creating relationships of dominance and dependency. Conversely, when giving and receiving occurs in right relationship on both the material and spiritual planes, it has the potential to catalyze a generative, spiraling dynamic beyond our wildest dreams.

PART IV

A Philanthropy4Life Initiative?

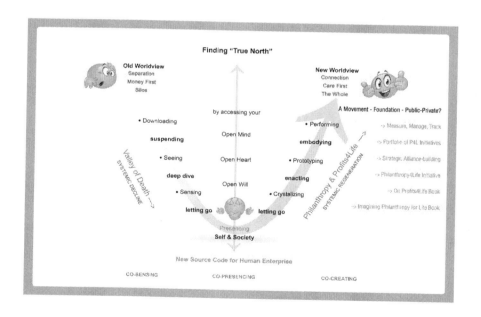

Chapter 15

True North for Humankind Revisited

Imagining Philanthropy for Life Authors

Y ou have now arrived at the concluding chapters of *Imagining Philanthropy for Life*. The preceding chapters invited you on a journey encompassing the proposition and rationale for transforming our being and doing in regard to philanthropy – an invitation to embrace our individual and collective True North based on truth, trust, and love.

True North was defined as our moral and spiritual direction aligned with the laws of the universe and nature. Embracing True North essentially holds the promise and lure of pointing our human enterprise on Earth in the direction of a more secure, peaceful, prosperous, and sustainable way of life. It can be thought of as reaching safe harbor after a voyage across tumultuous seas. True North symbolizes a truth that we can trust and bring to fruition if we mindfully make day-to-day decisions, small and large, based on universal love.

Part I developed True North as a way forward arising from deep-felt gratitude for the gift of life and our responsibility to cherish this gift.

- Experiencing our connectedness to a universal web of life from within, be it through meditation, prayer, or simply being in and working with nature, keeps our connections to True North lively.

- Choosing to apply Care First is no trivial, soft, New Age notion. It is where the rubber of our human enterprise, destiny, and manifested reality meets the road. Our individual and collective decisions determine whether we experience war or peace, insecurity or security, well-being or (dis)ease, and a sustainable or unsustainable future.

- In a fast, interconnected, exponentially changing world, we essentially have no choice but to be guided to True North by what flows from our hearts.

- All of the above must be grounded in our daily actions. To take up this challenge, it is imperative to reframe, reinvent, redirect, and reimagine philanthropy in full alignment with our innate attraction to True North.

- Philanthropy for Life seeks to accomplish this by internalizing "as above" and inviting you to embrace "so below" as a whole-system strategy for unleashing true love for humankind – a love that is secure, peaceful, sustainable, and flourishing.

- Philanthropy for Life's whole-system strategy proposes that money, time, talent, and creativity be invested in a life-giving, entrepreneurial ecosystem at the scale and urgency required to literally love to death humanity's most persistent challenges. Humanity finds itself in a "'valley of death" from which it can emerge victoriously if it redirects philanthropy and profits in support of life.

- Philanthropy for Life's rationale, goals, and desired metrics were outlined in a fair amount of detail while recognizing that judgement might have needed to be suspended for you to fully accept its practicality until more information was provided in subsequent chapters.

Part II juxtaposed our definition of True North with the deeply entangled past, present, and future of philanthropy. Highlights were:

- Philanthropy, which literally means "for the love of humankind," is deeply rooted as archetypical stories in belief systems worldwide. Humans everywhere know of similar, deeply resonating stories of Promethean fire and hope brought down from the heavens.

- Not unlike a form of global citizenship (as in everyone can be a philanthropist), these stories and myths collectively express the opportunity and responsibility to realize our full evolutionary potential.

- Philanthropy has lost much of its classical meaning, purpose, and potential impact. Individual philanthropy represents the bulk of our giving, and is typically connected to personally identified causes. Philanthropy by foundations and corporations is more strategic yet frequently unresponsive to root-cause needs, and relationships with recipients are more distant.

- Philanthropy as practiced today is invariably out of right relationship between giver and receiver – a lack of reciprocity, respect, and responsibility. By and large philanthropists (all of us) need to dare to care, take more risk, and become venture capitalists for good – in other words, be more fully engaged in private initiative for public good.

- Analysis of giving flows in the US and worldwide raises important questions as to the quantity and quality of our giving. The quantity has remained at an average of 2 percent of world GDP for the last 40 years, and the quality of the $370 billion in US giving flows that are directed to a whole-system embrace of life is negligible, hard to quantify, and thus difficult to track and manage.

- If the world we want is to become secure, peaceful, prosperous, and sustainable, the quality and quantity of our philanthropy must not only improve but also transform. The inconvenient truth is that philanthropy is enabled by and entangled with a profit-maximizing financial-economic system with significant fiscal drivers that perpetuate the continuous wholesale of the integrity of all life at the expense of future generations.

- It is this inherent contradiction of counteracting flows that needs to be resolved with courage and clarity in order to reset our course to True North based on the truth of that course, our trust in its wisdom, and our love for humanity.

Part III presented stories of transformation of self and society by innovators committed to finding their True North. Each story contributed to ways in which we can reimagine philanthropy.

- Susan Davis Moora opened our eyes to the highly effective workings of KINS Innovation Networks – her pioneering Trojan Horse of Love. *Imagining Philanthropy for Life* and our emerging Philanthropy4Life Initiative are in no small measure inspired by the KINS method and follow in the footsteps of a number of highly successful KINS networks.

- Stuart Valentine reminded us of the wealth-creating potential we all carry within. Once opened through meditation, these channels of opportunity allow us to integrate the fields of philanthropy and investing as one in order to unfold the gift of life through what are our dharmic destiny paths. Stuart considers nature to be the true "Central Bank" of our wealth and well-being. He introduced us to an integral investment model called the True Wealth Tree.

- Barbara Savage and Jyoti took us to the timeless world of indigenous wisdom, which should guide all our actions, such as the simplicity of paying close attention to reciprocity, respect, and responsibility to deepen all our relations. We are also reminded that first nations and first peoples are proven stewards and are essential partners sustaining the whole of life. Without them, the future of generations to come is likely bleak.

- Louis Bohtlingk wrote about the creation of a Care First world, where Care First, as opposed to Money First, governs all our decisions. He holds a compelling vision for a School of Care designed to coach humanity during its evolutionary, transformational process of letting go of Money First illusions in order to embrace fulfilling lives and careers with meaning and purpose based on the application of Care First.

- Bret Warshawsky and Andrea Harding explained the awakening of spiritual philanthropy and synergistic co-creation. Their Noomap platform provides for supporting, encouraging, and living a lifestyle of unconditional sharing and synergistic value exchange. Co-creators organically self-organize around reciprocal, altruistic communities in exchanging resources to support a fountain of gift consciousness and a gift civilization.

- Daniel Blaeuer wrote that only a new, reimagined philanthropy can foster a reenergized practice capable of unleashing the very love of humanity that is needed to address our collective human challenges in the twenty-first century. Reimagined philanthropy must return to the ethos of community, education, and responsible citizenship. It is accessible to all.

- Marilyn Levin discussed how various forms of flow funding are changing the face of philanthropy in important and creative ways. Flow Funding, for example, chooses visionaries, most of whom have never given money away before, to disburse funds in intuitive and heartfelt ways. It focuses equally on the process of giving and its effect on each flow funder and recipient. Flow funding is thought of as a healing-arts form of giving.

- Steven Lovink proposed Philanthropy for Life as a whole-system strategy to transform finance and grow true wealth. It is a call to action to mobilize, invest, measure, and track philanthropic funding flows directed towards catalyzing an entrepreneurial ecosystem that operates in service with the whole of life. When coupled with Profits4Life, both our philanthropy and profit-making can work in unison to creatively unlock private initiative for public good. Only then will we have embarked on a credible journey of investing in a secure, peaceful, prosperous, and sustainable future.

Chapter 16

Towards a New Era for America and the World

Steven Lovink

You are invited in this book to consider embracing Philanthropy for Life as a whole-system strategy that supports approaches for advancing systemic change that address the root causes of local-to-global challenges. It is tantamount to a global life insurance policy in case of systemic breakdown.

All of our challenges (and their solutions) have in common that they are mutually interdependent because of their intimate connection to our web of life. Whether one considers the world's big yet failing banking and finance system; our threatened ability to provide healthy, nutritious food to future generations of local and urban populations; the need to address increasing wealth gaps; declining trust in our systems of governance; true democracy at risk following the US Supreme Court's "Citizens United" decision; or of course resource constraints and climate change, humankind's enterprise can no longer afford to ignore that the silos within which we predominantly operate are somehow disconnected, insulated from cross-contagion effects, and not subservient to the larger truth of life's interconnectedness.

Digging deeper, we cannot but conclude that our problems are fundamentally about Care First versus Money First and whether or not our philanthropy and profits flow (or do not) in investment directions that foster peaceful, prosperous, and sustainable ways of life. Digging even more, we yearn for the vision, optimism, and hope to get the Herculean job done.

Four recently released books, coupled with associated emerging movements, deserve attention in this regard. Their proposed ways forward have much potential to synergize with the vision, optimism, and hope being offered by Philanthropy for Life. Here is an opportunity for collaborative, win-win acceleration of all such proposals. All tap into values and principles that bring out America's best. Each presents sustainable solutions for a purpose-driven nation that has lost its way. Each points to the need for grassroots "Promethean" civic leadership from within to overcome political gridlock and malaise by means of a range of community and entrepreneurial activities that serve a greater systemic whole – a more evolved entrepreneurial civilization operating in harmony with life.

The New Grand Strategy: Restoring America's Prosperity, Security, and Sustainability, by Mark Mykleby, Patrick Doherty, and Joel Makeower,[1] resulted from the assignment in 2009 by then Chairman of the Joint Chiefs of Staff, Admiral Mike Mullen, to devise a new grand strategy focused on America's twenty-first-century future and not its past. It had been 56 years since Dwight Eisenhower had defined the last grand strategy in the aftermath of World War II.

Mykleby and Doherty produced a white paper that laid out a strategy for recapturing America's greatness at home and abroad called *A National Strategic Narrative,* published by the Woodrow Wilson International Center for Scholars in 2011. It argued for elevating sustainability as a national strategic imperative. *The New Grand Strategy* takes this work further in the form of a business plan for America. Combining hard facts and profound truths based on economic analysis, demographic shifts, climate change, and resource scarcity, we are made aware of a $1.3 trillion annual business opportunity focused on private sector initiatives targeted at walkable communities, regenerative agriculture, and resource productivity. A vision for a new era for America and the peoples of all nations takes shape to propel discourse and action beyond divisive politics and partisan rhetoric to a pragmatic pathway to a prosperous, secure, and sustainable twenty-first century that transcends generations – with or without Washington's leadership.

Catalyzing and supporting a new American grand strategy for the twenty-first century is the mission of the Strategic Innovation Lab (SIL) based at Case Western Reserve University in Cleveland, Ohio. Mark Mykleby is co-director of SIL, implementing a top-down business-planning and bottom-up regional-initiatives framework that places economic and security logic at the center of a new national strategy. Taken together, these top-down and bottom-up approaches "capture, leverage, and amplify the economic opportunities that sustainability offers to Main Street USA." SIL's grand strategic framework is designed to show that all American citizens can shape the future of their country.[2]

What Then Must We Do Now?: Straight Talk about the Next American Revolution, by Gar Alperovitz, addresses the question "If you don't like capitalism and you don't like socialism, then what do you want?" As a historian and political economist, the author invites us into a timely discussion about democratizing the ownership of wealth to strengthen communities and our nation by means of local cooperatives, worker-owned companies, and independent businesses as well as larger publicly owned enterprises and revamped public institutions. It is a refreshing take on reinvigorating democracy and civic life by building a community-sustaining economy from the ground up. Careful analysis and intellectual grounding produces a vision and hope for "a next American Revolution," for which a proposed strategy and blueprint for action are rooted in the reality of the urgent need for transformational change of the system itself.[3]

The Next System Project was launched in 2015 by the Democracy Collaborative as:

> ...an ambitious multi-year initiative aimed at thinking boldly about what is required to deal with the systemic challenges the United States faces now and in coming decades. Responding to real hunger for a new way forward, and building on innovative thinking and practical experience with new economic institutions and approaches being developed in communities across the country and around the world, the goal is to put the central idea of system change, and that there can be a "next system," on the map.[4]

"The vision is that of a "Pluralist Commonwealth.""[5]

Sacred America, Sacred World: Fulfilling Our Mission in Service to All, by Stephen Dinan, presents a trans-partisan, evolutionary approach for enabling America to rise above political gridlock and bring out the best in all of us.[6] The following is from the book's press release:

> Dinan's solution calls for each side to grow up and evolve, rather than vilify each other and fight. Drawing on the findings of developmental psychology, Dinan shows how America can leave behind our adolescent need for winner-take-all politics, and adopt a constructive, patient, and *mature adult* approach to politics. This also requires that we confront and heal our buried traumas such as centuries of slavery as well as our genocide against Native Americans.[7]

Sacred America, Sacred World explores four ways that prevailing partisan divisions can be transcended and bridged for America to fulfill its higher mission to the nation and to the world. Developing a sacred worldview speaks to an emergent, more holistic and reverential way to experience our world. This sacred vision is already encoded in America's founding ideals and implied by an interdependent globalized world.

Evolving political leadership invites us to consider how we can become more whole as a people by healing the divisions that separate us, which are ultimately reflections of our fractured consciousness. The 100-percent solution is entering into a new era without leaving anyone behind. Creating innovative solutions includes considering how a combination of trans-partisanship and a sacred worldview can lead to more effective policies for family, school, community, and nation at necessary scales and even foster a peaceful, sustainable world.

Building an evolutionary movement includes creating an effective trans-partisan political movement that advances sustained change that addresses the fundamental need for evolving our country and the world. It explores how a global democracy can evolve as America's highest fulfillment and mission.

UBUNTU Contributionism: A Blueprint for Human Prosperity, by Michael Tellinger, proposes a new social structure for a new world in which everyone contributes their natural talents or acquired skills for the greater benefit of all in their community.[8] The concept of *contributionism* first emerged in 2005 out of research into ancient human history and how civilization has morphed over thousands of years. The research demonstrated that all ancient cultures embraced a philosophy that was largely identical in order to survive as isolated communities. The philosophy is mostly based on the ancient tribal structures of the African people, as well as many other native tribes of the world, albeit with adaptations for our times. It seeks to restore the rights of all the people to the people.

Organizing principles are that the country, land, roads, railways, waters, lakes, rivers, oceans, forests, mountains, skies, airwaves, and minerals (the "commons") belong to the people. Ubuntu is focused on uniting people across borders and the cultural divides imposed on humanity. Ubuntu Contributionism is laying the foundations for communities of abundance and prosperity on a beautiful planet of infinite abundance: "If it's not good for everyone, it's no good at all."

While Ubuntu is rooted in South Africa, it has increasingly broad international reach, and the movement has recently launched in the US. Ubuntu USA's aim is to move from a money-driven society to a society driven by people, their talents, and their passions for life, in which everyone contributes their natural talents or acquired skills to the greatest benefit of all in their community.

According to its media kit, Ubuntu USA's ambitious goals are to restructure the entire banking system to serve the people; establish a "People's Bank" that creates money for the people by the people, tax-free and interest-free; let scientists and inventors deliver a renewable source of free energy for everyone; support traditional healers and research scientists in finding alternative cures for all diseases; support farmers at every level in growing organic food; ban all genetically modified seeds; plant food gardens across the nation so that no person in the US ever goes hungry again; decentralize the government so people can govern themselves in their own communities, taking care of their own needs immediately, supported by the new People's Bank; and restructure the judiciary and the legal systems, to be written by the people for the people, unlike the unjust legal system we face in our courts today, which holds the rights of corporations above the rights of living, breathing human beings.[9]

On Intergenerational Banking, Finance, and Investment

It is safe to state that our prevailing Money First world system is inherently unstable and failing us. With still-fresh memories of the 2008 housing market crisis, which resulted in bailouts of banks too big to fail, trillions of dollars of quantitative easing by central banks, and a national and world economy that has still not found the ignition switch, one has to wonder what "unforeseen" event will trigger the next financial meltdown. Possibilities are numerous, and here are a few: enlarged conflicts and (resource) wars, drought and food crises, reset of the International Monetary Fund reserve currency, issuance of a global currency, natural disasters, terrorism, stranded fossil fuel assets of $25 trillion, civil unrest, revolt against digital currencies, and major health pandemics.

The US government is greatly indebted, as are many other governments, and faces one budgetary crisis after the next. Government is generally considered broken. In contrast, there are trillions of dollars available through private investment, such as an estimated $16 trillion in: corporate cash ($3.5 trillion), private equity and hedge funds ($10 trillion), and cash held by institutional investors ($2.5 trillion).[10] Notable, too, is that American retirement savings amount to some $24 trillion, that intergenerational wealth transfers between the WWII generation and Baby Boomers is pegged at $17 trillion, and that a stunning $30 trillion of wealth will transfer to the Millennial generation. Clearly there are tremendous sums of money sitting idle on the sidelines that need to be reinvested and could be deployed to support a whole-system strategy to transform finance and grow true wealth. The problem and solution is that a compelling long-term investment proposition for the future has been sorely missing. How can we build such a case?

A stubborn systemic design flaw in the DNA of our monetary system is perpetually creating financial wealth for the few while deteriorating the well-being of many, including the whole of life. Much of this financial wealth will ultimately evaporate in the form of stranded, phantom wealth if we consider and accept that our economic, social, natural, cultural, and spiritual stocks, flows, and resiliency (our "true wealth") will be further depleted until there is nothing left. This will happen unless a full-spectrum sustainability framework such as advocated by Mark Mykleby, Patrick Doherty, and Joel Makower in *The New Grand Strategy* reorients our banking, finance, and investment activities around self-organizing principles and values – an upgraded financial DNA that promotes a peaceful, sustainable, and flourishing way of life. This reorientation would benefit greatly, too, from Gar Alperovitz's vision for a "Pluralist Commonwealth," Stephan Dinan's vision for a "Sacred America, Sacred World" featuring evolved trans-partisan leadership, and Michael Tellinger's vision of Ubuntu Contributionism. To this list we could add the work of many others such as Hazel Henderson on transforming finance, Thera van Osch on "The Caring Economy," and David Korten on "A Living Economy for a Living Earth." They all contribute parts of yet a greater whole.

One could argue, as I do here, that a new era for America and the world is largely predicated on the successful emergence of an "Intergenerational Banking, Finance, and Investment" sector. Its mission should be to implement a new top-down and bottom-up whole-system financial strategy that operates in harmony with all life for the benefit of current and future generations. The vision would be that of a networked, public-private, collaborative forum to promote, advance, and catalyze not only our philanthropy but also our profits and investments in support of life. Such a forum would welcome all who hear its calling and could be resourced with funding, talent, and leadership that have the capacity to achieve necessary impact at scale.

The simple yet profound truth one can trust is that the love-centered rationale of our cosmology of connection and transformation, the ethics of care, and the case for Philanthropy for Life as humanity's True North made throughout this book apply equally well to profit-making, investments, and the creation of money. As soon as our philanthropy, profits, investments, and money creation are self-organized and governed based on a cosmic embrace of the whole of life, we will be heading to our True North.

If our current financial DNA is the root cause of humanity's predicament, can we redesign it at the point of its creation? While some believe that a world without money can one day be a reality, it seems reasonable to assume that for the foreseeable future we will demand money and currencies, including alternative currencies. The more fundamental challenge is to conceive of a new financial DNA that creates cosmically aligned money in service of love, care in action, and life. Money thus created enables the healing of people and planet as prosperity is shared instead of hoarded.

We have learned from the ongoing global financial crisis that the Federal Reserve (a privately owned entity), the European Central Bank, and their equivalents around the world can create (print) money out of thin air on behalf of governments to stimulate their economies. These monetary interventions are intended to inject the economy with necessary liquidity via the banking sector, set interest rates, create jobs, and facilitate economic growth.

Despite many trillions in quantitative easing, money is not flowing effectively to achieve its desired purpose, and remains largely stuck within the financial system. This is happening despite interest rates hovering at all-time lows, even *below* zero.

Creation of money results in an offsetting public debt, payable by governments. Such debts are ultimately guaranteed by ordinary citizens in the form of taxes to cover ever larger interest payments to private banks (which are too big to fail) on ever-mounting public debt. This works like a dream for the private banking, finance, and investment world for as long as their license to operate can be maintained, which may now be in jeopardy.

An Intergenerational Banking, Finance, and Investment Forum should assess how the US financial system's DNA can be effectively redesigned to deliver better results for tax-paying citizens who are the true underwriters of public debt, courtesy of their elected representatives in Congress. The forum might conclude that the creation of money should largely be controlled by public rather than private banks.

Ellen Brown, founder of the Public Banking Institute, would certainly recommend this. Public banks are premised on the idea that all the people, rather than just wealthy corporations and shareholders, have the right and responsibility to create value and issue credit. According to this institute there are now public banking initiatives, local organizers, and widespread discussions taking place all over the country about creating a public banking system, including in Washington, Oregon, California, Arizona, New Mexico, Colorado, North Carolina, Florida, Michigan, New York, New Jersey, Delaware, Maine, Illinois, Vermont, Hawaii, Pennsylvania, and the District of Columbia, as well as in Canada. But the forum would also develop pathways for both public and private banks to create money for public and private benefit in alignment with the new top-down and bottom-up financial grand strategy referred to above.

We are not necessarily faced with a choice between private banking, finance, and investment and public banking, finance, and investment, as long as the majority subscribe to issuing credit and creating value that contribute to a secure, peaceful, sustainable, and prosperous way of life. In other words, an Intergenerational Banking, Finance, and Investment Forum would collaboratively yet decisively point all noses True North.

The United States has, since its founding, always been recognized as a most generous nation. Despite that the philanthropy of the rich and famous so often captures media attention, we must not forget that the majority of giving comes from ordinary citizens (as do taxes). In this day and age everybody in the crowd can be and often is a philanthropist. Also consider the size of The Love Economy, mentioned earlier, which in combination with Mother Nature's productive, non-monetized capacity rivals if not exceeds the size of our monetized productive systems. Yet on the whole we have not become more generous as a percentage of GDP over the last 40 years. We have also committed a grave collective error by allowing ourselves to be separated from honoring the gift of life in so many ways, big and small. The annual value of just 17 ecosystem services delivered to us as gifts of life has been estimated at $125 trillion, more than one-and-a-half times annual global GDP of $74 trillion.[11] Ecosystem services are in serious decline almost everywhere. Good stewardship and governance of self and society based on self-organizing principles based on truth, trust, and love such as presented in this book must indeed become our True North.

Whether by design or unintended consequence, the stagnation of generosity and the decline in global well-being are the outcomes of a monetary and financial system that sacrifices a future of abundance for mostly private gain. It has now suffocated an otherwise naturally resilient circulatory and healthy web of life.

The world can still be regenerated by balancing economic, social, natural, cultural, and spiritual sources and flows. For this to happen at speed and scale, it is particularly important to apply the impulse of our philanthropic gifts and deliver them in a timely manner at the bottom of the U that both self and society are now experiencing. At that very point we must dedicate a larger portion of corporate profits to sustain the future of life. We must also lean hard into the truth that faith in fiat currency created out of thin air now hangs on to the fragile thread of life itself. We must thus create money to build a purpose-driven world that respects all life. A fruitful world economy (from *ecos*, meaning "home" in Greek) is one contained within safe planetary boundaries and social foundations that are in turn limited or enabled by our own conscious evolution.

Chapter 17

A New Worldview and Source Code

Louis Bohtlingk, Steven Lovink, Stuart Valentine

During the writing of *Imagining Philanthropy for Life* we engaged in highly generative dialogues among our team of authors. One of the many gifts that came out of this process was the mutual appreciation that our project has the potential of becoming more than a book. At a minimum we hope this book will open up an important ongoing dialogue with and among its readers. We are planning to facilitate this by means of a website, an online discussion forum, and a series of presentations by our team during upcoming conferences.

We believe the urgency, need, and opportunity to truly reimagine philanthropy are such that Philanthropy for Life's stated goals deserve to be co-created through a multiyear initiative in collaboration with all who read this book and for whom the bell tolls. What should bind us together coherently is a shared commitment to push for implementation of life's whole-system source code for unleashing true love for humankind – the resetting of our civilizational compass to True North.

Perhaps you might want to assist with this path-breaking effort. We hope *Imagining Philanthropy for Life* forms the seed for realizing the potential of an emergent initiative that might one day soon develop into a deeply inspiring movement, foundation, or public-private partnership for public benefit.

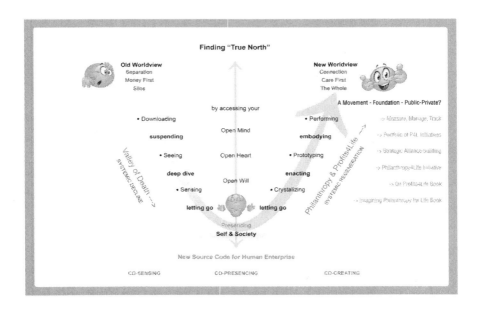

A Seven-Point Phased Strategic Plan

The road map towards the development, launch, and organic implementation of a forward-pulling strategic vision and plan for our Philanthropy4Life Initiative can be summarized as follows:

- **Phase 1:** Already ongoing and from which this book emerged, phase 1 entails the continuous presencing of our whole-system strategy to transform finance and grow true wealth by accessing our open minds, hearts, and wills. The process aims to refine the new source code for self and society, which is essentially to embed Philanthropy for Life's creative impulse as financial DNA and spark systemic transformation towards a new world view from within ourselves. A Philantropy4Life Stewardship Council composed of the authors of *Imagining Philanthropy for Life* and invited thought leaders is being established to guide the source code's development and conscious evolution following the KINS method and applying Theory U.

- **Phase 2:** Initiated in the fall of 2016, phase 2 focuses on the marketing and promotion of *Imagining Philanthropy for Life* nationally and internationally with the aim of reaching and engaging an ever-widening circle of readers. We invite them to plug in and play with Philanthropy for Life in order to foster new ways of being and doing and to grow awareness of its rationale and benefits. An engaging website supports these activities.

- **Phase 3:** The Philanthrop4Life Initiative will work hand in hand with Profits4Life. The former catalyzes flows of funds to communities and entrepreneurship in service with the whole of life, while the latter aims to recirculate profits from success ("Profits4Life") to support and grow an expanding entrepreneurial ecosystem that operates in harmony with life. The Philanthropy4Life Initiative will be enhanced by the release of *On Profits4Life: The Alchemy of Money, Love, and Life* in the second quarter of 2018, which it will help market and promote.

- **Phase 4:** Authors, stewards, and advisors dedicated to the development of the Philanthropy4Life Initiative will interact and convene meetings to prepare a business plan and funding strategy for its organizational architecture, staffing, launch, seed funding, ongoing funding, and implementation.

- **Phase 5:** Relationships with strategic implementation partners will be built to establish an Intergenerational Banking, Finance, and Investment Forum; develop a series of Give4Life Indices; attract venture development, finance, and fund-management expertise; issue an international call for proposals and launch contests for breakthrough initiatives that exemplify the application of Philanthropy for Life and Profits4Life; and appoint an experienced Philanthropy4Life Investment Advisory Committee.

- **Phase 6:** Phase 6 involves the assembly of an initial and expanding portfolio of breakthrough Profits4Life initiatives to be catalyzed with Philanthropy4Life funding flows. Candidate projects will be identified from within our network based on recommendations from our strategic partners and pursuant to the aforementioned call for proposals and contests for submission of breakthrough initiatives.

- **Phase 7:** Phase 7 will build trust in and branding of the Philanthropy4Life Initiative as a movement, foundation, public-private partnership, or institute for and on behalf of people in order to achieve its mission to transform finance and grow true wealth. We will seek to meet the highest standard in good governance, transparency, and accountability, including indices and benchmarks that monitor, track, and manage impactful performance.

A Whole-System Investment Opportunity

A key role of the Philanthropy4Life Initiative will be to connect flows of intentional giving (the supply of capital) in support of its mission to establish whole-system entrepreneurial initiatives that serve the larger community of life (the demand for capital). The initiative's capacity to successfully manage this challenge and reap the desired impact can grow and be organically adjusted following the dynamics of supply and demand for such investment capital.

- On the supply side, humankind should set itself aggressive but achievable goals. We believe a target of an additional 1 percent of global GDP in giving by 2025 (approximately $770 billion in current dollars) is achievable and would be a good start. This goal could be achieved through 0.1 percent annual increments over the next ten years. We would not be surprised if during this coming decade collective consciousness expands and demands that the target be adjusted upward to 10 percent or even more.

- On the demand side, we see a great and urgent need to support the realization of a secure, peaceful, sustainable, and prosperous way of life. The demand for capital to achieve such a society is estimated at many tens of trillions of dollars per year, as explained above. Much of this demand will be to secure capital in forms we are familiar with and that seek to maximize profits – in other words, business as usual.

- Philanthropy4Life initiatives will focus on serving the growing niche demands for investment capital in service with the whole of life. This demand would be driven by whole-system community and entrepreneurial enterprises that provide products and services that sustain all life, and its founders, owners, management, and organization as a whole would commit to the Profits4Life approach of reinvesting and recirculating profits from success to spark an upward, virtuous, systemic spiral of hope in support of a life-driven and purpose-driven entrepreneurial business ecosystem.

- We believe the pipeline of eligible initiatives may at first be modest; it is a new source code and financial DNA. But we are also confident that whole-system enterprise development will soon become a fast-growing sector and much more than a niche, for it represents the next frontier and nexus of evolutionary progress for humankind. Communities and entrepreneurs who recognize the opportunity of the new source code will over time gladly embrace the ability to get their products and services to market faster and with more success by adopting a business model that operates in harmony with life and caters to a growing market of increasingly conscious consumers.

Wouldn't everyone rather purchase a product or service from a company that cares for life visibly and verifiably through its commitment to a new world view? And in particular if the price and quality were comparable to or better than those of a competitor still committed to business as usual? In this way we can start small, yet transform self and society systemically from within at scale.

Chapter 18

Ten Ways to Engage with the Philanthropy4Life Initiative

Imagining Philanthropy for Life Authors

Journeys of transformation of self and society always start with those few first tiny steps. We have tried to plant a seed with this book as a gift to life to make that first step. So why shouldn't you also become a subtle philanthropic activist, a Trojan Horse of Love?

1. We invite you to help us spread the word by passing on this book to a family member, colleague, or friend. Our aim is to open hearts, minds, and wills everywhere across all sectors of society.

2. Purchase extra copies of *Imagining Philanthropy for Life* by taking advantage of our Buy One, Give One program and distribute them within your organization or community to contribute to the kindling of Philanthropy for Life within others.

3. Visit our website. Sign up, endorse our work, become an Ambassador4Life, "like" us, share links, receive our news, and access forthcoming online learning resources.

4. If you meditate or engage in contemplative practice or prayer, consider letting the images at the beginnings of Parts I through IV guide you to experiencing the inherent potential for a new world view. Discover how it can bring passion and purpose to your life.

5. If you are a teacher, educator, trainer, or coach, use this book to start a lively dialogue. Put the book on your reading list, be it recommended or required.

6. If you are a whole-system entrepreneur working with your community on breakthrough ideas, products, and services that are in service with the whole of life, connect with us. We like to celebrate stories of success and are interested in exploring how we can support each other.

7. If you are working in the financial sector, consider joining our Intergenerational Banking, Finance, and Investment Forum. Inspire, be inspired, and lead with passion and purpose.

8. If while reading this book you sensed the potential for a strategic alliance or potential collaboration with us, please contact us. It's all hands on deck to unleash true love for humankind!

9. Consider making a donation, small or large or anything in between. Be it money, talent, or time, it will greatly nourish Philantropy4Life Initiative's Promethean fire, optimism, and hope.

10. If you are a pope, king, queen, prince, or princess; an executive of a nation, corporate empire, big philanthropic foundation, or non-governmental organization; or are an otherwise noble, influential, philanthropic human being – *noblesse oblige*. Let's build a joint legacy!

May Philanthropy for Life by and for all (as in "everybody is a philanthropist" and "we are the ones") be the coming decade's Trojan Horse of Love. And if you still wonder, "What's love got to do with all this?" — well, everything; and it is written in the stars of a universe propelled by love!

Please connect with us via www.philanthropy4life.net.

Endnotes

Chapter 1: The Cosmology of Connection and Transformation

1. Simon Worrall. "How 40,000 Tons of Cosmic Dust Falling to Earth Affects You and Me". National Geographic. 2015. http://news.nationalgeographic.com/2015/01/150128-big-bang-universe-supernova-astrophysics-health-space-ngbooktalk

Chapter 2: Care First – Our Ethical Compass and Light

1. Thera van Osch. "The Economy of Care". 2015. http://www.docfoc.com/the-economy-of-care-an-economic-approach-for-a-sustainable-future-thera-van
2. David Korten. *Change the Story, Change the Future: A Living Economy for a Living Earth.* Oakland, California: Berrett-Koehler Publishers. 2015.

Chapter 3: Philanthropy for Life – Humanity's True North

1. Will Steffen, et al. "Planetary Boundaries: Guiding Human Development on a Changing Planet." *Science* vol. 347 no.6223. 2015.
2. C. Otto Sharmer. *Theory U: Leading from the Future as It Emerges.* Oakland, California: Berrett-Koehler Publishers. 2016.
3. Presencing Institute. "Theory U". 2015. https://www.presencing.com/theoryu
4. Trucost. "Universal Ownership: Why Environmental Externalities Matter to Institutional Investors". 2012. http://www.unepfi.org/fileadmin/documents/universal_ownership_full.pdf

5. Lawrence Mishel and Alyssa Davis. "Top CEOs Make 300 Times More than Typical Workers". 2015. http://www.epi.org/publication/top-ceos-make-300-times-more-than-workers-pay-growth-surpasses-market-gains-and-the-rest-of-the-0-1-percent

6. GrantCraft. "Funding Indigenous Peoples: Strategies for Support". Foundation Center, in partnership with the International Funders for Indigenous Peoples. 2015. http://internationalfunders.org/wp-content/uploads/2016/02/2015-Funding-Indigenous-Peoples-Strategies-for-Support.pdf

Chapter 4: True Love for Humankind through Time and Space

1. Catalogue for Philanthropy. "What Is Philanthropy?" 2008. http://www.philanthropydirectory.org/about-us/philanthropy-explained

2. Classical Literature. "Ancient Greece – Aeschylus – Prometheus Bound". 2009. http://www.ancient-literature.com/greece_aeschylus_prometheus.html

3. Susmita Chakraborty and Anup Kumar Das. *Collaboration in International and Comparative Librarianship*. Hershey, Pennsylvania: IGI Global, 2013.

4. South India Cinema Magazine (southdreamz.com). "Surya – A Man of Good Heart and Countless Deeds". 2013. http://www.southdreamz.com/56126/surya-a-man-of-good-heart-and-countless-deeds

5. Quotes (quotes.net). "Buddha: If you knew what I know about the power of giving..." http://www.quotes.net/quote/3534

6. George McCully. *Philanthropy Reconsidered: Private Initiatives – Public Good – Quality of Life*. Bloomington, Indiana: AuthorHouse, 2008.

7. Steven T. Newcomb. *Pagans in the Promised Land*. Golden, Colorado: Fulcrum Publishing, 2008.

8. National Philanthropic Trust. "Charitable Giving Statistics". 2016. https://www.nptrust.org/philanthropic-resources/charitable-giving-statistics

9. The Giving Pledge. "Frequently Asked Questions". 2013. http://givingpledge.org/faq.aspx

10. Charities Aid Foundation. "CAF World Giving Index 2015: A Global View of Giving Trends". https://www.cafonline.org/docs/default-source/about-us-publications/caf_worldgivingindex2015_report.pdf?sfvrsn=2

11. The Giving Institute. "Giving USA Annual Report". 2015. http://www.givinginstitute.org/?page=GUSAAnnualReport

12. Helen Brown. "Cracking the 2% Nut". 2016. The Helen Brown Group https://www.helenbrowngroup.com/cracking-the-2-percent-nut

13. Suzanne Perry. "The Stubborn 2% Giving Rate". The Chronical of Philanthropy. 2013. https://www.philanthropy.com/article/The-Stubborn-2-Giving-Rate/154691

14. Tim Mullaney. "Why Corporate CEO Pay Is So High, and Going Higher". CNBC.com. 2015. http://www.cnbc.com/2015/05/18/why-corporate-ceo-pay-is-so-high-and-going-higher.html

15. Floyd Norris. "Corporate Profits Grow and Wages Slide: Off the Charts". *The New York Times*. 2014. http://www.nytimes.com/2014/04/05/business/economy/corporate-profits-grow-ever-larger-as-slice-of-economy-as-wages-slide.html

Chapter 5: Challengers Facing the Art and Science of Giving

1. Phil Buchanan. "Big Issues, Many Questions". 2016. The Center for Effective Philanthropy. http://research.effectivephilanthropy.org/big-issues-many-questions

2. Chaya Shucat. "Eight Degrees of Giving". 2005. http://www.chabad.org/library/article_cdo/aid/256321/jewish/Eight-Degrees-of-Giving.htm

3. Will Steffen, et al. "Planetary Boundaries: Guiding Human Development on a Changing Planet." *Science* vol. 347 no.6223. 2015.

4. Kate Raworth. "A Safe and Just Space for Humanity: Can We Live within the Doughnut?" *Oxfam Policy and Practice: Climate Change and Resilience* 8.1 (2012): 1-26.

5. Brian Dumaine. "Can a (Billionaire) Hedge Fund Manager Fix Income Inequality?". *Fortune.* 2015. http://fortune.com/2015/09/23/paul-tudor-jones-just-capital-survey

6. Dan Pallotta. *Charity Case: How the Nonprofit Community Can Stand Up For Itself and Really Change the World.* Hoboken, New Jersey: Jossey-Bass, 2012.

7. Peter Kim and Jeffrey Bradach. "Why More Nonprofits Are Getting Bigger". 2012. Stanford Social Innovation Review. https://ssir.org/articles/entry/why_more_nonprofits_are_getting_bigger

8. Paul Kedrosky. "The Constant: Companies that Matter". Ewing Marion Kauffman Foundation. 2013. http://www.kauffman.org/~/media/kauffman_org/research%20reports%20and%20covers/2013/05/companiesthatmatter.pdf

9. Indigenous Peoples' Literature. "Native American Ten Commandments". 1993-2016. http://indigenouspeople. net/tencomm.htm

10. Bill Gates. "Technology Means Everyone Can Be a Philanthropist". *The Huffington Post*. 2013. http://www.huffingtonpost.com/bill-gates/giving-tuesday_b_4385393.html

11. Ryan Scott. "The Rocket Fuel for Your Philanthropy Is Technology". *Forbes*. 2015. http://www.forbes.com/sites/causeintegration/2015/11/05/the-rocket-fuel-for-your-philanthropy-is-technology/#292418f922dc

12. Ken Wilber. "Ken Wilber". *Integral Life*. 2013. https://www.integrallife.com/contributors/ken-wilber

13. Ken Wilber. *Integral Spirituality: A Startling New Role for Religion in the Modern and Postmodern World* Boulder, Colorado: Shambhala, 2007.

14. Michael Dowd. "Ten Commandments to Avoid Extinction: Reality's Rules". YouTube. 2016 http://www.youtube.com/watch?v=YJj33_omnkg

15. Bruce Lipton. *The Biology of Belief: Unleashing the Power of Consciousness, Matter and Miracles*. Mountain of Love Publishing, 2005.

16. Tom Campbell. "Tom Campbell and Bruce Lipton: Two Scientists 'See the Same World'". 2013. https://www.youtube.com/watch?v=BjDQzCq6FdM

17. Jair Robles. "Evolution by Choice, Not Chance: Interview with Barbara Marx Hubbard". *SuperConsciousness Magazine*. 2012. http://www.superconsciousness.com/topics/discover/evolution-choice-not-chance

18. Ilia Delio. *Making All things New: Catholicity, Cosmology, Consciousness.* Maryknoll, New York: Orbis Books, 2015.

19. Love Made Visible. "Ervin Laszlo". 2015. http://www.lovemadevisible. eu/examples/ervinlaszlo

20. Ervin Laszlo "The Giordano Bruno GlobalShift University and Its Commitment to the Young People of the World". 2012. http:// www.tandfonline.com/doi/pdf/10.1080/02604027.2012.638237

21. Wikipedia. "Don Edward Beck". 2013. https://en.wikipedia.org/ wiki/Don_Edward_Beck

Chapter 6: Emerging Solutions in Search of True North

1. Forbes Insights. "2015 BNP Paribas Individual Philanthropy Index". https://cdn-actus.bnpparibas.com/files/upload/2015/02/27/ docs/2015-bnpp-wm-philantropyindex-report.pdf

2. Kasia Moreno. "The Top Five Most Promising Trends in Philanthropy". *Forbes.* http://www.forbes.com/sites/forbesinsights/2015/03/02/the-top-five-most-promising-trends-in-philanthropy/#75f204a25ec0

3. "The Future of Philanthropy". Various contributors. *The Nation,* August 15-22, 2016.

4. Global Impact Investing Network research team. "2016 Annual Impact Investor Survey". 2016. https://thegiin.org/assets/2016%20 GIIN%20Annual%20Impact%20Investor%20Survey_Web.pdf

5. Morgan Simon. "Impact Investing: The Benefits and Challenges of an Emerging Field". RSF Social Finance. 2012. http://rsfsocialfinance. org/2012/10/19/impact-investing-emerging-field

6. The Giving Pledge. http://givingpledge.org

7. The Synergos Institute. "Global Philanthropists Circle". http:// www.synergos.org/philanthropistscircle/gpcbrochure.pdf

8. Green America Center for Sustainability Solutions. http:// centerforsustainabilitysolutions.org

9. Mark R. Kramer. "Catalytic Philanthropy". *Stanford Social Innovation Review*, Fall 2009. https://ssir.org/articles/entry/ catalytic_philanthropy

10. Giving Circles Network. "Why We're Here". http://givingcircles.org

11. Forbes Insights. "2015 BNP Paribas Individual Philanthropy Index". https://cdn-actus.bnpparibas.com/files/upload/2015/02/27/ docs/2015-bnpp-wm-philantropyindex-report.pdf.pdf, retrieved 07/02/2016

Chapter 8: The Alchemy of Transformational Investing

1. The Forum for Sustainable and Responsible Investment. "US SIF Releases Report on Impact of Sustainable Investment". http://www. ussif.org/blog_home.asp?Display=69

2. Gaia & Eros. "Hazel Henderson's Cake Diagram Never Made More Sense". 2008. https://gaiaeros.com/2008/11/11/hazel-hendersons- cake-diagram-never-made-more-sense

3. Charles Eisenstein. *Sacred Economics: Money, Gift, and Society in the Age of Transition*. Berkeley, California: Evolver Editions, 2011.

Chapter 12: Reimagining Philanthropy as Community, Education, and Citizenship

1. George McCully. *Philanthropy Reconsidered: Private Initiatives – Public Good – Quality of Life*. Bloomington, Indiana: AuthorHouse, 2008.

Chapter 14: On Philanthropy and Profits4Life

1. Susan Davis Moora. *The Trojan Horse of Love: KINS Innovation.* 2015. http://www.kinsinnovation.org/remarkable-friends-of-kins/the-trojan-horse-of-love-free-ebook

2. Ricardo Bayon, J. Steven Lovink, and Wouter J. Veening. "Financing Biodiversity Conservation." 2000.

3. Rhodri Davies. "Giving Unchained: Philanthropy and the Blockchain". Charities Aid Foundation. 2015. https://www.cafonline.org/docs/default-source/about-us-publications/givingunchained-philanthropy-and-the-blockchain.pdf?sfvrsn=4

Chapter 16: Towards a New Era for America and the World

1. Mark Mykleby, Patrick Doherty, and Joel Makeover. *The New Grand Strategy: Restoring America's Prosperity, Security, and Sustainability in the 21st Century.* New York City: St. Martin's Press, 2016.

2. Strategic Innovation Lab. Weatherhead School of Management. 2015. https://weatherhead.case.edu/centers/fowler/strategic-innovation

3. Gar Alperovitz. *What Then Must We Do? Straight Talk about the Next American Revolution.* Democracy Collaborative. 2014. http://democracycollaborative.org/content/what-then-must-we-do-straight-talk-about-next-american-revolution

4. The Next System Project. "About the Next System Project". 2011. http://thenextsystem.org

5. The Next System Project. "The Pluralist Commonwealth". You Tube. 2016. https://www.youtube.com/watch?v=yEEzripANUQ

6. Stephen Dinan. *Sacred America, Sacred World: Fulfilling Our Mission in Service to All.* Newbury, Massachusetts: Hampton Roads Publishing, 2016.

7. *Sacred America, Sacred World: Fulfilling Our Mission in Service to All* press release. 2016. http://www.sacredamerica.net/press

8. Michael Tellinger. *UBUNTU Contributionism – A Blueprint for Human Prosperity*. Cape Town, South Africa: Zulu Planet Publishers, 2013.

9. Ubuntu USA. Ubuntu USA Media Kit. September 2016.

10. Mark Mykleby, Patrick Doherty, and Joel Makeover. *The New Grand Strategy: Restoring America's Prosperity, Security, and Sustainability in the 21st Century*. New York City: St. Martin's Press, 2016.

11. Robert Costanza et al. "Changes in the Global Value of Ecosystem Services." *Global Environmental Change* 26 (2014): 152-158.

Bibliography

Alperovitz, Gar. *What Then Must We Do? Straight Talk about the Next American Revolution*. Democracy Collaborative. 2014. http://democracycollaborative.org/content/what-then-must-we-do-straight-talk-about-next-american-revolution

Bayon, Ricardo, J. Steven Lovink, and Wouter J. Veening. "Financing Biodiversity Conservation." 2000.

Brown, Helen. "Cracking the 2% Nut". 2016. The Helen Brown Group. https://www.helenbrowngroup.com/cracking-the-2-percent-nut/

Buchanan, Phil. "Big Issues, Many Questions". 2016. The Center for Effective Philanthropy. http://research.effectivephilanthropy.org/big-issues-many-questions

Campbell, Tom. "Tom Campbell and Bruce Lipton: Two Scientists 'See the Same World'". 2013. https://www.youtube.com/watch?v=BjDQzCq6FdM

Catalogue for Philanthropy. "What Is Philanthropy?" 2008. http://www.philanthropydirectory.org/about-us/philanthropy-explained

Center for Sustainability Solutions. http://www.centerforsustainabilitysolutions.org

Centerpoint Investment Strategies. http://www.centerpointinvesting.com

Chakraborty, Susmita and Anup Kumar Das. *Collaboration in International and Comparative Librarianship*. Hershey, Pennsylvania: IGI Global, 2013.

Charitable Giving in America. http://nccs.urban.org/nccs/statistics/Charitable-Giving-in-America-Some-Facts-and-Figures.cfm

Charities Aid Foundation. "CAF World Giving Index 2015: A Global View of Giving Trends". https://www.cafonline.org/docs/default-source/about-us-publications/caf_worldgivingindex2015_report.pdf?sfvrsn=2

Clark, Jeff. "Nine Predictions for Philanthropy in 2016". 2016. https://philanthropynw.org/news/nine-predictions-philanthropy-2016

Classical Literature. "Ancient Greece – Aeschylus – Prometheus Bound". 2009. http://www.ancient-literature.com/greece_aeschylus_prometheus.html

Costanza, Robert, et al. "Changes in the Global Value of Ecosystem Services." Global Environmental Change 26 (2014): 152-158.

Davies, Rhodri. "Giving Unchained: Philanthropy and the Blockchain". Charities Aid Foundation. 2015. https://www.cafonline.org/docs/default-source/about-us-publications/givingunchained-philanthropy-and-the-blockchain.pdf?sfvrsn=4

Delio, Ilia. *Making All things New: Catholicity, Cosmology, Consciousness.* Maryknoll, New York: Orbis Books, 2015.

Dinan, Stephen. *Sacred America, Sacred World: Fulfilling Our Mission in Service to All.* Newbury, Massachusetts: Hampton Roads Publishing, 2016.

Dowd, Michael. "Ten Commandments to Avoid Extinction: Reality's Rules". YouTube. 2016 http://www.youtube.com/watch?v=YJj33_omnkg

Dumaine, Brian. "Can a (Billionaire) Hedge Fund Manager Fix Income Inequality?". *Fortune.* 2015. http://fortune.com/2015/09/23/paul-tudor-jones-just-capital-survey

Eisenstein, Charles. *Sacred Economics: Money, Gift, and Society in the Age of Transition.* Berkeley, California: Evolver Editions, 2011.

Ferris, David. "Technology: Inside Solar's Secret Society". *Energy-Wire,* Sept. 6, 2016.

Flow Funding. http://flowfunding.org

Forbes Insights. "2015 BNP Paribas Individual Philanthropy Index". https://cdn-actus.bnpparibas.com/files/upload/2015/02/27/docs/2015-bnpp-wm-philantropyindex-report.pdf

Forum for Sustainable and Responsible Investment. "US SIF Releases Report on Impact of Sustainable Investment". http://www.ussif.org/blog_home.asp?Display=69

Foundation Center. "Funding Indigenous Peoples: Strategies for Support". in partnership with the International Funders for Indigenous Peoples. 2015.

Foundation Strategy Group (FSG). http://www.fsg.org

Gaia & Eros. "Hazel Henderson's Cake Diagram Never Made More Sense". 2008. https://gaiaeros.com/2008/11/11/hazel-hendersons-cake-diagram-never-made-more-sense

Gates, Bill. "Technology Means Everyone Can Be a Philanthropist". *The Huffington Post.* 2013. http://www.huffingtonpost.com/bill-gates/giving-tuesday_b_4385393.html

Giving Circles Network. "Why We're Here". http://givingcircles.org

Giving Institute, The. "Giving USA Annual Report". 2014. http://www.givinginstitute.org/?page=GUSAAnnualReport

Giving Pledge, The. http://givingpledge.org/faq.aspx

Global Impact Investing Network. https://thegiin.org/assets/2016%20GIIN%20Annual%20Impact%20Investor%20Survey_Web.pdf

Goldschmeding Foundation. www.goldschmedingfoundation.org

Grantmakers in the Arts. "Philanthropy in the World's Traditions". Edited by Warren F. Ilchman, Stanley N. Katz, and Edward L. Queen II. 1998. http://www.giarts.org/article/philanthropy-worlds-traditions

Greater Horizons. "A Brief History of Charitable Giving" (infographic). https://www.greaterhorizons.org/sites/default/files/history-of-philanthropy.png

Green America Center for Sustainability Solutions. http://centerforsustainabilitysolutions.org

Hurst, Aaron. *The Purpose Economy: How Your Desire for Impact, Personal Growth and Community Is Changing the World.* Boise, Idaho: Elevate, 2014.

Indie Philanthropy Initiative. https://indiephilanthropy.org

Indigenous Peoples' Literature. "Native American Ten Commandments". 1993-2016. http://indigenouspeople.net/tencomm.htm

Institute for Environmental Security. http://www.envirosecurity.org

International Funders for Indigenous People. http://internationalfunders.org

Kania, John and Mark Kramer. "Collective Impact". Stanford Social Innovation Review, Winter 2011. http://ssir.org/articles/entry/collective_impact

Kedrosky, Paul. "The Constant: Companies that Matter". Ewing Marion Kauffman Foundation. 2013. http://www.kauffman.org/~/media/kauffman_org/research%20reports%20and%20covers/2013/05/companiesthatmatter.pdf

Kelly, Marjorie. *Owning Our Future: The Emerging Ownership Revolution.* San Francisco, California: Berrett-Koehler Publishers. 2012.

Kim, Peter and Jeffrey Bradach. "Why More Nonprofits Are Getting Bigger". 2012. Stanford Social Innovation Review. https://ssir.org/articles/entry/why_more_nonprofits_are_getting_bigger

KINS Innovation Networks. http://www.kinsinnovation.org

Korten, David. *Change the Story, Change the Future: A Living Economy for a Living Earth*. San Francisco, California: Berrett-Koehler Publishers. 2015.

Kosmos Journal for Global Transformation. http://www.kosmosjournal.org

Kramer, Mark. "Catalytic Philanthropy". *Stanford Social Innovation Review*, Winter 2011. http://ssir.org/articles/entry/collective_impact

Lapham, Lewis H. "Pennies from Heaven". *Lapham's Quarterly* Summer 2015 http://www.laphamsquarterly.org/philanthropy/pennies-heaven

Laszlo, Ervin "The Giordano Bruno GlobalShift University and Its Commitment to the Young People of the World". 2012. http://www.tandfonline.com/doi/pdf/10.1080/02604027.2012.638237

Levin, Marilyn. *Experiential Activities for a Better World: A Guidebook for Facilitators, Teachers, Trainers and Group Leaders*. CreateSpace Independent Publishing Platform. 2010.

Lipton, Bruce. *The Biology of Belief: Unleashing the Power of Consciousness, Matter and Miracles*. Mountain of Love Publishing, 2005.

Love Made Visible. "Ervin Laszlo". 2015. http://www.lovemadevisible.eu/examples/ervinlaszlo

Lovink, Steven. "On Living Business". *Kosmos Journal for Global Transformation*. 2015. http://www.kosmosjournal.org/article/on-living-business

McCully, George. *Philanthropy Reconsidered: Private Initiatives – Public Good – Quality of Life*. Bloomington, Indiana: AuthorHouse, 2008.

Mishel, Lawrence and Alyssa Davis. "Top CEOs Make 300 Times More than Typical Workers". 2015. http://www.epi.org/publication/top-ceos-make-300-times-more-than-workers-pay-growth-surpasses-market-gains-and-the-rest-of-the-0-1-percent

Moora, Susan Davis. *The Trojan Horse of Love: KINS Innovation*. 2015. http://www.kinsinnovation.org/remarkable-friends-of-kins/the-trojan-horse-of-love-free-ebook

Moreno, Kasia. "The Top Five Most Promising Trends in Philanthropy". http://www.forbes.com/sites/forbesinsights/2015/03/02/the-top-five-most-promising-trends-in-philanthropy/#75f204a25ec0

Mr. Y. "A National Strategic Narrative". Woodrow Wilson International Center for Scholars. 2011. https://www.wilsoncenter.org/sites/default/files/A%20National%20Strategic%20Narrative.pdf

Mullaney, Tim. "Why Corporate CEO Pay Is So High, and Going Higher". CNBC.com. 2015. http://www.cnbc.com/2015/05/18/why-corporate-ceo-pay-is-so-high-and-going-higher.html

My Big Toe. https://www.my-big-toe.com

Mykleby, Mark, Patrick Doherty, and Joel Makeover. *The New Grand Strategy: Restoring America's Prosperity, Security, and Sustainability in the 21st Century*. New York City: St. Martin's Press, 2016.

Nation, *The*. "The Future of Philanthropy". Various contributors. August 15-22, 2016.

National Philanthropic Trust. "Charitable Giving Statistics". 2016. https://www.nptrust.org/philanthropic-resources/charitable-giving-statistics

Newcomb, Steven T. *Pagans in the Promised Land*. Golden Colorado: Fulcrum Publishing, 2008.

Next System Project, The. "About the Next System Project". 2011. http://thenextsystem.org

Norris, Floyd. "Corporate Profits Grow and Wages Slide: Off the Charts". *The New York Times*. 2014. http://www.nytimes.com/2014/04/05/business/economy/corporate-profits-grow-ever-larger-as-slice-of-economy-as-wages-slide.html

Pallotta, Dan. *Charity Case: How the Nonprofit Community Can Stand Up For Itself and Really Change the World*. Hoboken, New Jersey: Jossey-Bass, 2012.

Peace Through Commerce. http://www.peacethroughcommerce.org

Perkins, John. *The World Is As You Dream It: Teachings from the Amazon and Andes*. Rochester, Vermont: Destiny Books, 1994.

Perry, Suzanne. "The Stubborn 2% Giving Rate". The Chronical of Philanthropy. 2013. https://www.philanthropy.com/article/The-Stubborn-2-Giving-Rate/154691

Philanthropy Network. http://www.philanthropynetwork.org

Planetary Security Initiative. http://www.planetarysecurity.nl

Presencing Institute. "Theory U". 2015. https://www.presencing.com/theoryu

Public Banking Institute. http://www.publicbankinginstitute.org

Raworth, Kate. "A Safe and Just Space for Humanity: Can We Live within the Doughnut?" *Oxfam Policy and Practice: Climate Change and Resilience* 8.1 (2012): 1-26.

Robles, Jair. "Evolution by Choice, Not Chance: Interview with Barbara Marx Hubbard". *SuperConsciousness Magazine*. 2012. http://www.superconsciousness.com/topics/discover/evolution-choice-not-chance

Sahtouris, Elisabet. "Welcome". Lifeweb. http://www.sahtouris.com

Scott, Ryan. "The Rocket Fuel for Your Philanthropy Is Technology". *Forbes*. 2015. http://www.forbes.com/sites/causeintegration/2015/11/05/the-rocket-fuel-for-your-philanthropy-is-technology/#292418f922dc

Sharmer, Otto C. *Theory U: Leading from the Future as It Emerges*. Oakland, California: Berrett-Koehler Publishers. 2016.

Shucat, Chaya. "Eight Degrees of Giving". 2005. http://www.chabad.org/library/article_cdo/aid/256321/jewish/Eight-Degrees-of-Giving.htm

Simon, Morgan. "Impact Investing: The Benefits and Challenges of an Emerging Field". RSF Social Finance. 2012. http://rsfsocialfinance.org/2012/10/19/impact-investing-emerging-field

South India Cinema Magazine (southdreamz.com). "Surya – A Man of Good Heart and Countless Deeds". 2013. http://www.southdreamz. com/56126/surya-a-man-of-good-heart-and-countless-deeds

Stars Foundation. http://www.starsfoundation.org.uk

Steffen, Will, et al. "Planetary Boundaries: Guiding Human Development on a Changing Planet." *Science* vol. 347 no.6223. 2015.

Stockholm Resilience Centre. "Planetary boundaries". 2016. http:// www.stockholmresilience.org/research/planetary-boundaries.html

Strategic Innovation Lab. https://weatherhead.case.edu/centers/fowler/ strategic-innovation

Synergos Institute. "Global Philanthropists Circle". http://www.synergos. org/philanthropistscircle/gpcbrochure.pdf

Tellinger, Michael. *UBUNTU Contributionism – A Blueprint for Human Prosperity*. 2016. Cape Town, South Africa: Zulu Planet Publishers, 2013.

Trucost. "Universal Ownership: Why Environmental Externalities Matter to Institutional Investors". 2012. http://www.unepfi.org/ fileadmin/documents/universal_ownership_full.pdf

van Osch, Thera. "The Economy of Care". http://www.docfoc.com/ the-economy-of-care-an-economic-approach-for-a-sustainable-future-thera-van

Wilber, Ken. "Ken Wilber". Integral Life. 2013. https://www.integrallife. com/contributors/ken-wilber

Wilber, Ken. *Integral Spirituality: A Startling New Role for Religion in the Modern and Postmodern World*. Boulder, Colorado: Shambhala, 2007.

Worrall, Simon. "How 40,000 Tons of Cosmic Dust Falling to Earth Affects You and Me". *National Geographic*. 2015. http://news.nationalgeographic.com/2015/01/150128-big-bang-universe-supernova-astrophysics-health-space-ngbooktalk

Appendix A

The Creation of **KINS** Innovation Networks

Susan Davis Moora

At the age of 38 I was a Chicago bank vice president active in the women's movement who had tried and failed to start a national women's news magazine. Sad with that experience, I suggested to the other seven women on our magazine team an idea that could refresh the hope we'd had with the magazine. I suggested we start a leadership network of Chicago's 100 top women across all fields from finance to religious organizations to artists to doctors. The answer was YES!

For a year we researched to find the top women, vetted them, invited their ideas for the network's highest purpose, raised some expense money, and launched the network in 1979. Almost effortlessly, operating principles evolved that were sharply different from business as usual. The way I describe them is:

- Our strategy is generosity.

- Everyone does what we love to do and do well without charge.

- A deal is a good deal when it is good for all concerned, especially Earth.

- Everyone has equal status and equal time at the mic.

- All information is available to all members all the time.

Quickly the highest opportunities and biggest obstacles for women in Chicago were addressed, with solutions launched and funded. The joy of meeting one's peers ran so deep that attendance never fell below robust.

After the pain of the magazine's failure, I could not bear to go home after the founders' retreat for what we called The Chicago Network, which thrives today (www.thechicagonetwork.org). Each person was giving our all to each other, while opening to receive. Rather than the competition that I felt so restricted the world of finance, there was plenty of joy, laughter, helpfulness, and strategic information to go around for everyone.

I decided that night that whatever I had to do to make it happen, I would never let go of having a love-network like this in my life.

And I never have.

Over the last 40 years of this networking, my role has been to create a core founders' network, inspire them to create a mission statement, create a larger support group around this mission, do the research to identify which 30 to 40 sectors could most further the mission, find the most respected servant-leaders in each sector, hear their ideas for the network, and organize a three-day founders' retreat for launching the network. Once launched at the retreat, I'd fade back to regular membership like everyone else so network leaders could self-identify at the retreat with the support of all.

Inspired by the network's mission, everyone contributed what they loved to do and do well and nothing else, everyone working without pay. This method has proved to be effective in achieving progress, efficient in the use of resources, and highly enjoyable and meaningful for participants... at minimal expense.

Imagine a For-Profit Company Gifting Its Proprietary Innovation to a Nonprofit!

After developing the first few "innovation networks," I created a for-profit called Capital Missions Company (CMC) in 1990 to house this work, rather than a nonprofit, because I had a strong desire for this effort to be self-supporting! This strategy worked and KINS Innovation Networks, as it was now called, prospered. With its success, however, I did need expansion capital, and several venture firms in my KINS Investor Circle wanted to provide it.

However, I believe in a good deal for all and not just a good deal for those with money. I also did not want to keep proprietary the innovation method we were developing – I wanted the whole world to have access to it. As I puzzled over this quandary, a close investor/philanthropist friend, Diana Beliard, offered to make the needed capital available to CMC, and I gratefully accepted.

A few years later, one of my social-investor networks reneged on an agreement to assure repayment of a bank loan CMC had obtained to launch them. In this crisis another investor/philanthropist friend,

Virginia Rogers, stepped forward to gift the needed funds for the loan repayment. From there CMC was able to thrive, spreading KINS Innovation Networks while making enough to cover expenses, make some contributions, and enjoy a small return.

In 2012, I was ready to retire at 70, and netted a profit from the sale of my US home, since I was happily living in Vilcabamba, Ecuador. Holding the check in my hand, I remembered my lifetime dream of becoming a philanthropist. Now I could be! Further, a student at my first "Teaching KINS" program, Marilyn Levin, had so fallen in love with the method that she had left her global nonprofit to work free spreading the KINS method. After six months of her excellent work, I was feeling uncomfortable about the unfairness of that. Since Alisa Gravitz, founder of Green America, had been invaluable to KINS by facilitating innumerable KINS networks once launched, Green America was the only nonprofit to which I considered gifting the KINS method, funding, and name. I gifted my $100,000 to RSF [Rudolf Steiner Foundation] Social Finance, also a close collaborator, and then to Green America. I breathed a sigh of relief that Marilyn could be paid, and I felt deep joy to be a philanthropist.

In my mind this proved that philanthropic gifts to for-profit companies as venture capital investments can yield high and lasting social impact. Rather than hoarding the breakthrough for those who can afford it, it can be gifted widely throughout the world for all humankind, just as is happening with KINS Innovation Networks now.

If you are inspired to dig deeper into this adventure of KINS Innovation Networks, please read my book, *The Trojan Horse of Love*, gifted at www.capitalmissions.com/TrojanHorseOfLove.pdf.

Here is one story from the book that I wish to share: About 14 years ago, I fell seriously ill. For months I could eat little but smoothies. Finally I gleaned from various healers I serendipitously met that to heal, I needed a "cleansing program," something I had never heard of. By "coincidence" my husband, Walter, and I were vacationing in Kona, Hawaii, when I was drawn into a funky bookstore and then inspired to open a book called *The Wisdom of Hawaiian Elders*. Next I was inspired to open to a page about a Kona healer called Auntie Margaret Machado who was celebrated worldwide for her... CLEANSING PROGRAMS.

By a miracle, she was giving one in a few days, and an attendee had dropped out, making my participation possible. Walter returned to the States and I duly began the program. After only a day of discomfort, I began healing deeply and fully. My favorite practice was at sunset, when we would each find our own private spot of meditation and review the day, forgiving ourselves for anything we had done to hurt anyone else in thought, word, or deed, and forgiving each other person who had hurt us in thought, word, or deed. Called Ho'oponopono, it was profound indeed. I had a number of extremely powerful experiences during these sunset meditations.

On the 10th day of 12, I sat down for my sunset reverie and this time went into a state I cannot easily explain. All I know is that it became clear that my life purpose was to serve as a Trojan Horse of Love within finance, for finance was the heart of Earth's problems and needed to be transformed from greed to love.

It also became clear that this challenge would take me to my limit, for I would have to freeze my heart while training my mind to incredible discipline in order to establish credibility within finance. I knew I had three gifts to help meet this challenge – excellent health, the ability to always hear my inner voice, and, most important, the ability to find numerous kindred spirits to assist me with this path.

I also knew that having the father and mother I had was a huge asset as well. My father was a master of all the aspects of business, so I was prepared for the discipline of finance. And my mother was a master of all the forms of love, so I learned how to release love in ways appropriate to different situations.

All of this brought an unbelievably deep sense of gratitude and connection, and I moved more deeply into the experience of clarity and grace.

I now look back and see that starting in my childhood, I have been in training as a Trojan Horse of Love. I remember when I was eleven and a friend got polio. I heard that the Jimmy Fund was searching for a polio cure, and I organized the whole neighborhood to do a circus to donate money to the Jimmy Fund. This was my first experience organizing a large group of people to serve a cause higher than myself, and this has turned out to be one of the key goals in my life.

Then I see that the training continued when I finally maneuvered my way into finance. I found that the energy field in financial offices was too strict and analytical for me to speak of love there. I realized that I could identify people who might also be Trojan Horses of Love and gather them away from the office where I could share very deeply and personally. In this way I was able to help people find their destiny paths. Then they were able to give birth to initiatives that brought more momentum to social investing and to support each other in playing stronger roles in growing that industry.

Now you have the story of why I am alive... and why I focused on transforming finance.

Now I must ask you...

Are you, too, a Trojan Horse of Love? If yes, imagine your highest possibilities for using what you love to do and do well to restore Earth and her people! Might it serve you to co-create a KINS Innovation Network? Or to join one that exists? You'll find them described at www.KINSinnovation.org.

Do come connect with us.

Appendix B

KINS Innovation Networks – A Primer

Susan Davis Moora

The information below serves any group of conscious folk in service to Earth and its people in achieving their missions. See additional stories and videos at www.KINSinnovation.org.

What Are KINS Innovation Networks?

KINS Innovation Networks are self-organizing networks of key, collaborative, high-integrity leaders in widely diverse fields who come together by invitation to achieve inspiring innovations while enjoying their kindred spirits. These networks leverage existing "conscious sustainability" initiatives to manifest a whole-system design based on the understanding that we are all one.

You are probably asking, "If there have been 40 successful KINS Innovation Networks launched over 40 years, why have I never heard of them?" The answer is that most of these networks of servant-leaders focus on manifesting the desired social change and not on teaching others their innovation method.

Success Stories of Highest-Impact KINS Innovation Networks

When Robert Sherriff of Hong Kong decided his life mission was "making solar happen for the world," he flew to meet me in Wisconsin to see if the KINS method could do that. Within six months we had identified 40 key servant-leaders of high status who represented the 40 sectors of making solar happen that we felt were most important.

We convened them and they identified the top 20 challenges and the top 20 opportunities for solar. They then took assignments based on their expertise and manifested several breakthroughs within months. One was to inspire the three competing solar organizations to become one and come to the major annual solar meeting with a shared agenda, which did get adopted. The main solar research institute then contributed free of charge a number of employees to create a document quantifying how solar could become the leading energy source in the world – after the energy industry had agreed to dismiss this idea. Within a year the energy industry had reversed its position based on the data documented.

One year later we were told that at the same time we started our KINS network, a leading global consulting firm in energy had set a budget of $1 million to create a board of advisors on solar to also bring solar center stage in the industry. One year later they had found only four experts willing to participate *if* time and expenses were paid and none of the $1 million had been raised. The project was abandoned. Other KINS success stories are described at www.KINSinnovation.org.

What Are the KINS Operating Principles? (Each KINS network customizes these to serve their purposes.)

- Our strategy is generosity and our intention is wonder.

- A deal is a good deal when it is good for all concerned, especially Earth.

- Everyone does what we love to do and do well without charge… and little else.

- We sit at the table of unknowing and co-create with Spirit/God and each other for the highest good for all concerned.

- When someone gets upset, we go within to ask what within us is asking to be healed… and later we bring the story of that healing back to the group to enrich the field.

- Everyone gets equal time at the mic and we return each others' calls and emails promptly.

- All information is available to all members all the time.

The KINS Criteria for Choosing Members (Each KINS network customizes these to serve their purposes.)

- have high credibility in their field

- give back the most in their field

- have a reputation for integrity

- have advanced collaboration skills

- have some kind of heartfelt spiritual practice and believe that we are all one

- are passionate about the network's mission

A KINS Network Is a Natural System

- works like nature works

- organizes around constituencies

- holds a strategy of generosity

- creates an optimal energy field

- uses a simple creation process

- practices core operating principles to create a unique, efficient culture

- creates breakthrough solutions

Steps for Forming a KINS Innovation Network

1. Craft your mission: make it daunting, measurable, and inspiring!

2. Choose your KINS type (see www.KINSinnovation.org for our spectrum diagram for KINS types).

3. Choose your sectors (The KINS method is a whole-system method, so choose comprehensively... ideally 30 to 40 different sectors.)

4. Identify members and invite them into your KINS network after ensuring they are aligned with the KINS principles.

5. Plan for a founders' retreat, for a traditional KINS network, or set up bi-weekly calls for a virtual KINS network.

6. Co-create network design for success of your particular mission.

7. Implement network design (innovating and co-creating as you go).

The Description of the Founders' Retreat (Each KINS network customizes it to serve their purposes.)

The founders' retreat begins after dinner on a Friday night, when members gather in a circle and tell a story about when they most trusted their intuition to take risks and find their destiny path based on their values. This shifts the usual competitive energy field to excitement about "our highest possibilities" as a group.

On Saturday morning members brainstorm their highest possibilities for manifesting their missions and the biggest obstacles they face. Highly creative collaborations are manifested and given their respected positions within the various constituencies that are important to the mission that has been crafted. These challenges are explored, along with a heart-based design for the evening's activities, depending on the network's purpose.

By Sunday, a very deep level of trust and creativity has been reached, so that in an hour or two the members agree on issues like legal structure, governance, membership, priorities, and self-funding.

KINS Innovation Networks Range from Highly Spiritual to Highly Rational

Throughout its history, each set of KINS founders has settled on an approach ranging from highly spirit-based to highly rational. The wide range within the over 40 KINS Innovation Networks that have existed since the method was developed prove that we can trust the founders to create the resonant energy field that works for them.

What KINS Innovation Networks Have Failed?

Some KINS networks date back to 1979 and flourish today, while others ended when their goal was achieved. A few ceased meeting before their purpose was fulfilled due to unexpected developments. One was called the Tipping Point Network (TPN), the purpose of which was to bring key leaders in 40 different niches of sustainability into collaboration. While TPN members made more than $3 million in grants to strategic projects in their first three years, they then disagreed about whether to have only one major shared goal or to have everyone's key goals honored. This led to an agreement that they would discontinue meeting and each refocus their efforts on manifesting sustainability in their own watersheds. They all do this now, continuing to stay in touch with the members they grew closest to.

Another example is our program at Green America called KINS for Philanthropists Manifesting Their Missions. Those in the first year's program (2013) helped us design how to make the 40 years of KINS experiences into a coherent teaching program. They grew very close personally and most of them stayed in touch in different ways.

However, their success in starting their KINS networks varies from wild success (see Louis Bohtlingk's story about his Care First KINS Innovation Network) to barely starting.

In summary, the KINS experience benefits all, even if in unexpected ways. Often the best things come directly out of the very worst things, just as in life; just like this book... because the first-year group had various levels of success while this third-year group is not only manifesting its missions, but published this book.

Made in the USA
Lexington, KY
13 April 2018